REVISED AND UPDATED

TOTAL FORGIVENESS

REVISED AND UPDATED

TOTAL FORGIVENESS

R.T. KENDALL

CHARISMA
HOUSE

Most Charisma House Book Group products are available at special quantity discounts for bulk purchase for sales promotions, premiums, fund-raising, and educational needs. For details, write Charisma House Book Group, 600 Rinehart Road, Lake Mary, Florida 32746, or telephone (407) 333-0600.

Total Forgiveness by R. T. Kendall
Published by Charisma House
Charisma Media/Charisma House Book Group
600 Rinehart Road, Lake Mary, Florida 32746
www.charismahouse.com

Library of Congress Catalog Card Number: 2002107082
International Standard Book Number: 978-1-59979-176-0

This book was previously published as *Total Forgiveness* by Hodder & Stoughton, ISBN 0-340-75639-X, copyright © 2001.

This publication is translated in Spanish under the title *Perdón total*, copyright © 2002 by R. T. Kendall, published by Casa Creación, a Charisma Media company. All rights reserved.

E-book ISBN: 978-1-59979-821-9

11 12 13 14 — 12 11 10 9
Printed in the United States of America

To Melissa

CONTENTS

FOREWORD

Here is the kind of message for which you have been waiting. This is not a book about forgiveness; the church libraries throughout Christendom are filled with volumes on this familiar topic. Sunday school lessons and sermons have been entreating hearers for generations to heed and to practice this basic Christian virtue.

Dr. R. T. Kendall supplies the clue in the very title of this important work: *Total Forgiveness*, which is achieving God's greatest challenge.

What makes this message so powerful is the fact that it comes to grips with the unavoidable concept of totality. To most finite human beings, the very notion of "allness" is formidable. Isn't that an attribute that belongs to God alone? The "omnis"—omnipotent, omnipresent, omniscient—are to be ascribed exclusively to Jehovah, aren't they?

Is the author extreme when he postulates emphatically that we are not only to forgive—but to forgive totally? No, he is just being biblical. Jesus Himself laid down the imperative to His disciples: "Be ye therefore perfect, even as your Father which is in heaven is perfect" (Matt. 5:48, KJV). No commandment in all of Scripture could be more explicit.

Are you forgiving totally...completely...utterly...absolutely...unconditionally...entirely...wholly? That is how Jesus forgives the sinner, and He expects no less from us. More than that, He makes it the foundation of our prayer life: "If ye forgive not men their trespasses, neither will your Father forgive your trespasses" (Matt. 6:15, KJV).

What message could be more timely than one that calls upon us today, as this book does, to forgive totally the grievances that seem to be ripping nations apart all around this troubled globe? If the various races, nationalities, and ethnic groups who are creating chaos and fomenting warfare with their enemies could be brought to forgive—to forgive totally—themselves, their tragic histories, the injustices that they have suffered in the past, and the hatreds that have hardened into virtual idolatries, we could be on the way to a more peaceful world.

I agree with Dr. Kendall that this is his most important book. And I agree with others who feel passionately that it is a book that should be read around the world.

—D. James Kennedy, PhD
Senior Minister, Coral Ridge Presbyterian Church
Fort Lauderdale, Florida

FOREWORD

ONE OF THE greatest subjects of the third millennium will be the relationship between the developed countries of the West and the developing countries in the third world, especially those in Africa.

A new world order has emerged that requires global mediation—a mediation whose main objective would be to contribute to the solution of ethnic conflicts within nations as well as conflicts between nations, and also to contribute to the promotion of world economic growth, development, and welfare. Some of us who have been involved in the practical mediation of these conflicts have come to the stark realization that nations, just as individuals, need to *forgive* each other for the past exploitation and suppression of their weaker neighbors. The nations of Africa are just one example of this. For a people group who has been so traumatized by the ravages of the cold war and colonialism; for a people who is seeking to come to terms with their history of oppression, conflict, and disagreement; for a people who has reached the rock bottom of despair and despondency, *there can be no future without forgiveness.*

It is in this context that I have found Dr. R. T. Kendall's book

Total Forgiveness to be immensely timely and appropriate at this particular juncture in our human history. It is a book that should be read by every race and nation in the world. Many atrocities have been committed and continue to be committed by various people groups in the name of politics or even religion; these currently include the conflicts in Rwanda, Bosnia-Herzegovina, Kosovo, Ireland, Sudan, Angola, Liberia, Somalia, Israel, and the Middle East, to mention only a few. There is much forgiveness that is needed.

It is important to look at the past, for, as the great American philosopher George Santayana once said, "Those who cannot remember the past are condemned to repeat it." But that does not mean that we should view the past with unforgiveness or bitterness in our hearts. R. T. Kendall has taught us through this book that bitterness, however much we feel it is justified, will only consume our souls and ultimately achieve nothing. We must therefore learn to forgive, even if we never forget.

Nelson Mandela is perhaps the best example in the twentieth century of a man who has taught us how to forgive. After twenty-seven years of political incarceration—the longest serving political prisoner in the world at that time—he emerged unscathed and told his people to forgive their oppressors and focus on the future and on building a new, united nation. In spite of the devastating trauma of apartheid, Mandela chose the path of forgiveness and reconciliation rather than the policy of revenge and vindictiveness. The world expected that a ghastly bloodbath would overwhelm South Africa, but this did not happen. South Africans managed an extraordinarily peaceful transition between governments and avoided a major ethnic and racial war. I am grateful to God who enabled me to play a role in that reconciliation and forgiving process.

In another part of the world, the Arab-Israeli conflict has continued for such a long time because it is based on the policy of instant, mutual retaliation—an eye for an eye and a tooth for a tooth. But in the final analysis, the parties in this terrible conflict will have to sit down around a table and negotiate a peaceful and lasting agreement—an agreement based on give and take, and based on reconciliation and forgiveness rather than retributive justice.

Clearly, the world has been waiting for such a book as *Total Forgiveness*, and R. T. Kendall has done humanity a great service in writing it.

—PROFESSOR WASHINGTON A. J. OKUMU
NAIROBI, KENYA

PREFACE

EVERY AUTHOR PROBABLY thinks that his or her latest book is the best or most important, and I am no different. This book, out of all the books I have written, is by far the one that has the greatest potential to heal the human heart. I do pray that this book will exceed all expectations for every person who reads it. It is designed to set people free.

I want to thank Rob Parson, Julia Fisher, Susan Periman, Michael Schluter, and Lyndon Bowring for reading the manuscript. These friends have been an invaluable encouragement to me by their pertinent suggestions and loving support. My thanks to Sheila Penton who typed the manuscript, and to Barbara Dycus and Deborah Moss, my editors at Charisma House, for their patience and help.

Dr. D. James Kennedy, senior minister of Coral Ridge Presbyterian Church in Fort Lauderdale, Florida, has kindly written the foreword to the American edition. I most warmly thank him for his endorsement and the powerful manner in which he has written. We both share a reformed theological perspective and a deep conviction that Christians must live in total forgiveness. Dr. Kennedy is the architect and founder of Evangelism Explosion, which has had a tremendous impact all over the world, but especially on my wife, Louise, and me particularly. We are so honored that he has joined us in this effort to show the joy and blessing of living in total forgiveness.

I also thank Professor Washington Okumu of Nairobi, Kenya, for his foreword to both the British and American editions. He came to see us in London a few years ago to say that this message had changed his life and even led him to do what he did in South Africa. We felt that American readers would appreciate his contribution. A student of Harvard and Cambridge, Professor Okumu studied under Dr. Henry Kissinger, among others. They later became friends and worked together to bring peace and reconciliation to South Africa. Professor Okumu's greatest legacy is that he was able to bring together former President F. W. de Klerk, Chief Mangosuthu Buthelezi, and Nelson Mandela and broker peace between them when Dr. Kissinger and Lord Carrington had failed to do so. This was one of the greatest miracles of the twentieth century, and Professor Okumu was almost certainly the main force responsible for averting a civil war in South Africa.

This book is lovingly dedicated to our daughter, Melissa. She knows what it is to suffer deep hurts, but also what it means to forgive—totally.

—R. T. Kendall
Key Largo, Florida
www.rtkendallministries.com

INTRODUCTION

"RT, you must totally forgive them. Until you totally forgive them you will be in chains. Release them, and you will be released."

No one had ever talked to me like that in my life. But those words, spoken to me unexpectedly by my friend Josif Tson of Romania, are among the most important words anybody has ever personally shared with me. "Faithful are the wounds of a friend" (Prov. 27:6, KJV).

The June 5, 2000, issue of London's *Daily Express* carried an article with this headline: "Can You Learn to Forgive?" It began with the following declaration: "Bearing a grudge can hold you back and even damage your health."[1] The writer of the article, Susan Pape, had interviewed Dr. Ken Hart, a lecturer at Leeds University, who had been running the "world's first forgiveness course"—a seminar designed to help people forgive their enemies and let go of grudges. Participants ranged from a jilted husband to victims of burglary and bullying. All had one thing in common: they were angry and bitter, and they wanted revenge.

This was not, as far as I know, a Christian course. Evidently it was a case of people doing something biblical without even realizing it. It is one indication that the world is starting to recognize the merits of a lifestyle of forgiveness. Unfortunately, Christians may be lagging behind. I myself was one who was unable to forgive for much of my life.

Most of us have times in our lives when we are pushed to our limits as to how much we are called to forgive. I remember what happened to me with such clarity. I have vowed not to retell this story, but suffice it to say I had never been hurt so deeply, before or since. The wrong I believe was done to me affected just about every area of my life: my family, my ministry, my very sense of self-worth. I felt at times like Job when he cried, "I have no peace, no quietness; I have no rest, but only turmoil" (Job 3:26); or like David when he prayed, "Answer me quickly, O Lord; my spirit fails. Do not hide your face from me or I will be like those who go down to the pit" (Ps. 143:7). I doubt that those who brought this situation upon me had any idea what I went through, and I pray they never will.

I blush to admit that those words from Josif Tson were spoken to me after I became the minister of Westminster Chapel. I, of all people, shouldn't have needed such a word. Nobody should have had to tell a mature minister of the gospel of Christ the most obvious and fundamental teaching of the New Testament. But there I was in the ministry of our Lord Jesus Christ, filled with so much hurt and bitterness that I could hardly fulfill my duties. I am almost ashamed to confess this, but I share it with you for two reasons: first, to show how gracious God has been to me in spite of my anger and self-pity, and second, to encourage you to walk in forgiveness toward others.

Astonishingly, before the reprimand from my friend, my unforgiving spirit had not bothered me all that much. If you had reminded me of Jesus's words that we should "love one another" (John 13:35) or of that petition in the Lord's Prayer, "Forgive us our debts, as we also have forgiven our debtors" (Matt. 6:12), I would have replied, "Of course I know about that." I assumed that since nobody is perfect and we all sin in some measure every day, the bitterness in my heart was no worse than any other person's transgression. Moreover, I thought, God fully understood and sympathized with my particular circumstances. In other words, I rationalized my attitude and behavior.

"He compassionately but soberly rebuked me and would not let me off the hook."

But mercifully, the Holy Spirit spoke to me that day through Josif's words. At first I was angry; I felt hemmed in. But it was a pivotal moment for me, and it changed my life. I was never the same again.

To be honest, I had only told Josif of my problem because I thought I would get sympathy from a man I deeply respected and whom I thought would be on my side. I expected him to put his arm on my shoulder and say, "RT, you are right to feel so angry! Tell me all about it. Get it out of your system."

But no! He compassionately but soberly rebuked me and would not let me off the hook.

Those words came to me during the greatest trial I had ever had until that time. I couldn't discuss it with my friends or family members, but because Josif was from Romania and was far removed from the situation, I was able to tell him everything.

"Is that all?" he asked when I finished my story.

"Yes, that's it," I said.

And then came those remarkable words—spoken in his Romanian accent: "You must totally forgive them."

"I can't," I replied.

"You can, and you must," he insisted.

Unsatisfied with his response, I tried to continue. "I just remembered. There is more. What I didn't tell you..."

"RT," he interrupted, "you must totally forgive them. Release them, and you will be set free."

It was the hardest thing I had ever been asked to do. What I write about in this book is far easier said than done. I repeat, it was the hardest thing I had ever been asked to do, but it was also the greatest thing I had ever been asked to do.

An unexpected blessing emerged as I began to forgive: a peace came into my heart that I hadn't felt in years. It was wonderful. I had forgotten what it was like.

God's peace had come to me years before—on October 31, 1955, when driving my car one Monday morning from my church in Palmer, Tennessee. Readers of my book *The Sensitivity of the Spirit* (Charisma House, 2002) may recall some of the story. I was on my way back from my student pastorate to Trevecca Nazarene College in Nashville. As I drove down the road, I could sense the Lord Jesus literally interceding for me at the right hand of the Father. I had never felt so loved. Jesus was praying for me with all His heart. The next thing I remember—an hour later—was hearing Jesus say to the Father, "He wants it." I heard the Father's voice reply, "He can have it." At that moment it felt as if liquid fire were entering my chest. I remembered John Wesley's words, "I felt my heart strangely warmed."[2] I felt an incredible peace that is impossible to describe. The person of Jesus was more real to me than anything or anyone else around me.

This feeling lasted for several months, but eventually I lost it. Now this peace and sense of Jesus's nearness was beginning to come back—all because I was setting those people free, forgiving them, letting them off the hook.

However, if I allowed myself to think about what those people did, I would get churned up inside. I would say to myself, "They are going to get away with this. This is not fair! They won't get caught. They won't be found out. Nobody will know. This is not right!" And the sweet peace of the Lord left again.

I began to notice an interesting cycle. When I allowed the spirit of total forgiveness to reign in my heart, the peace would return; but when I would dwell with resentment on the likelihood that they wouldn't get caught, the peace would leave.

I had to make an important decision: Which do I prefer—the peace or the bitterness? I couldn't have it both ways. I began to see that I was the one who was losing by nursing my attitude of unforgiveness. My bitterness wasn't damaging anyone but myself.

When we are bitter, we delude ourselves into thinking that those who hurt us are more likely to be punished as long as we are set on revenge. We are afraid to let go of those feelings. After all, if we don't make plans to see that justice is done, how will justice be done? We make ourselves believe that it is up to us to keep the offense alive.

This is a lie—the devil's lie. "Do not take revenge, my friends, but leave room for God's wrath, for it is written: 'It is mine to avenge; I will repay,' says the Lord" (Rom. 12:19). We only hurt ourselves when we dwell on what has happened to us and fantasize about what it will be like when "they" get punished. Most of all, we grieve the Holy Spirit of God, and this is why we lose our sense of peace.

> "I had to make an important decision: Which do I prefer—the peace or the bitterness?"

I have come to the conclusion that the primary way we grieve the Spirit in our lives is by fostering bitterness in our hearts. I say this because it is the first thing the apostle Paul mentions after warning us not to grieve the Spirit:

> And do not grieve the Holy Spirit of God, with whom you were sealed for the day of redemption. Get rid of all bitterness, rage and anger, brawling and slander, along with every form of malice. Be kind and compassionate to one another, forgiving each other, just as in Christ God forgave you.
>
> —Ephesians 4:30–32

It is also my experience that the quickest way I seem to lose inner peace is when I allow bitterness to reenter my heart. It's not worth it! I made a decision for inner peace. But I found that I had to carry out that decision by a daily commitment to forgive those who hurt me, and to forgive them totally. I therefore let them utterly off the hook and resigned myself to this knowledge:

- ▹ They won't get caught or found out.
- ▹ Nobody will ever know what they did.
- ▹ They will prosper and be blessed as if they had done no wrong.

What's more, I actually began to will this! I prayed for it to happen. I asked God to forgive them. But I have had to do this every day to keep the peace within my heart. Having been on both sides, I can tell you: the peace is better. The bitterness isn't worth it.

I write this book to encourage anyone who has had a problem with forgiving those who have hurt them, however deeply. I write this to help such people see the real reasons to forgive. Many people who read this book will have been through far worse than what I have experienced. But I have come to believe that the only way to move beyond the hurt and go forward in life is through total forgiveness. My prayer is that this book will change lives as my own was changed by Josif's loving rebuke.

I am convinced that this theme of total forgiveness is perhaps more crucially needed at this present moment than nearly any other teaching in the Bible. I say that for a number of reasons. First, whenever I preach the message of total forgiveness, there is a tremendous response. No sermon or theme I *ever* touch on comes close to the chord that is struck when I share on this subject. The response tells me that there is a terrific need for this message—even among Christians.

Second, when I return to this theme in my own church, even if I taught on it only a few weeks before, people respond as if they have never heard the message! This matter of getting rid of bitterness and totally forgiving one another is difficult to deal with.

I sometimes think it would be good if I preached this message every week!

> Having been on both sides, I can tell you: the peace is better. The bitterness isn't worth it.

Third, it is evident that I myself never felt sufficiently bothered by the unforgiveness I was harboring in my heart. Why? I have asked this question many times. I surely knew that this was Jesus's message. So why was I not gripped by my need to forgive? Why did I need the reprimand of a man who had lived behind the iron curtain? Did the Christians in Eastern Europe have an understanding of forgiveness that we in the West did not? Why do we not emphasize this message in our society?

I have read hundreds of sermons by the Puritans and the Reformers, but I cannot recall being told by them I must totally forgive or otherwise grieve the Holy Spirit. Godly though my own parents were, I cannot say this was something I was consciously taught at home. Not a single mentor that I can recall emphasized this as a lifestyle. On the contrary, I can remember being told: "Treat them with contempt." "Distance yourself from them." "Give them a cold shoulder." "Teach them a lesson." "They must be punished." Or other suggestions of that sort.

A fourth reason that the message of forgiveness is so timely in our day is that a growing number of informed people have recently discerned the need for further teaching on the subject. In a recent issue of *Christianity Today* with the bold words "The Forgiveness Factor" emblazoned across the front cover, writer

Gary Thomas reckons that this teaching has been greatly overlooked. Thomas cites theologian Lewis Smedes as one of the first to emphasize this—in 1984! Professor Robert Enright, president of the International Forgiveness Institute, who describes himself as an "evangelical Catholic," has commented that prior to Lewis Smedes's *Forgive and Forget* (1984), "If you collected every theological book about person-to-person forgiveness [as opposed to divine-human forgiveness], you could hold them all in one hand."[3] If this is true, although it doesn't excuse my attitude, it would help explain my own lack of awareness.

Some people marvel that a doctrine that seems so obvious in Scripture could apparently lie dormant, untaught for hundreds of years. But this should cause those of us who are church leaders to repent, not only for neglecting to teach forgiveness, but also for not putting it into practice in our own lives. Had this teaching been the emphasis and lifestyle of all of us who are in church leadership, there might not have been the division, hurt, and strife that have characterized many Christian circles. Though these strivings may often be described as a doctrinal battle for truth, so often the veneer is paper thin, and underneath are the age-old jealousies, petty agendas, and sheer humanness that affect us all.

Fifth, social scientists are discovering that forgiveness may help lead to victims' emotional and even physical healing and wholeness. As recently as the early 1980s, Dr. Glen Hamden went to the University of Kansas library and looked up the word *forgiveness* in *Psychological Abstracts*. He couldn't find a single reference. But things are changing. Former President Jimmy Carter, Archbishop Desmond Tutu, and former missionary Elisabeth Elliot have been promoting a $10 million "Campaign for Forgiveness Research," established as a nonprofit corporation to attract donations that will support forgiveness research proposals. In 1998 the John Templeton Foundation awarded research grants for the study of forgiveness to twenty-nine scholars,[4] and one of the primary discoveries of these studies is that the person who gains the most from forgiveness is the person who does the forgiving. Should this surprise us?

Although forgiveness has positive psychological—and even physical—benefits, this book is not about the results of psychological or sociological research. It is wholly about biblical teaching—about the spiritual blessing that comes to those who take Jesus's teaching of total forgiveness seriously. In a word, it is about receiving a greater anointing.

Because forgiving those who have hurt us severely can be a very difficult task—especially when trust is shattered—Michelle Nelson has chosen to speak of degrees, or different types, of forgiveness.[5] She has listed three categories:

1. Detached forgiveness—there is a reduction in negative feelings toward the offender, but no reconciliation takes place.

2. Limited forgiveness—there is a reduction in negative feelings toward the offender, and the relationship is partially restored, though there is a decrease in the emotional intensity of the relationship.

3. Full forgiveness—there is a total cessation of negative feelings toward the offender, and the relationship is fully restored.

I have chosen to speak of total forgiveness, if only because that is the expression my friend Josif Tson used with me. But this book is also about total forgiveness *even if there is not a restoration of the relationship.* One must totally forgive those who will not be reconciled.

> "The person who gains the most from forgiveness is the person who does the forgiving."

Even if there is no reconciliation, there can still be total forgiveness. This may even apply to the forgiveness of those who are no longer alive. This forgiveness must happen in the heart, and when it does, peace emerges—with or without a complete restoration of the relationship. What matters is that the Holy Spirit is able to dwell in us ungrieved, able to be utterly Himself. The degree to which the Holy Spirit is Himself in me will be the degree to which I am like Jesus and carry out His teachings.

As a medical doctor, one of the most important problems that I encounter among my patients is that of bitterness, resentment, and unforgiveness. It is a major reason why people don't heal. This book offers extremely practical information and refer many of my patients to it for reading. It is the best book that I have seen on the subject of forgiveness and I highly recommend it to everyone.

—"drken47"
Bowie, MD

1

WHAT IS TOTAL FORGIVENESS?

Father, forgive them, for they do not know what they are doing.

—Luke 23:34

WE ALL HAVE a story to tell. As you begin to read this book, you may think it is impossible to forgive your unfaithful husband or wife. You may feel you cannot forgive your abusive parent. You may feel you cannot forgive what was done to your son or daughter. How can we forgive the church leader who took advantage of his position? What about the person who lied to us or about us, or the person who believed those lies? The list of potential offenses is endless. There are rapists out there. Child abusers. Murderers. Often closer to home, there are unkind or unloving relatives and former close friends who have become enemies.

Forgiving Those Who Have Hurt Our Loved Ones

I received a heartrending letter from a couple who had heard me teach on the subject of total forgiveness a few years ago. They told me what their son-in-law had done to their daughter and grandchildren. It was an awful story. "Are you saying we must totally forgive our son-in-law?" they asked. That was a hard question to answer. But I had to tell them the truth: yes, they must learn to forgive. My heart went out to them. I can only imagine the pain they have experienced. But total forgiveness is the only way they will ever find freedom and release from the offense.

I have received many other letters that describe everything from infidelity to incest to rape to lying and slander. It is enough to make me consider very carefully indeed what I preach and write in this book. People experience real pain when they or someone they love is hurt by another person. It is often harder to forgive when the one who has been hurt is someone you love deeply, especially your child. I find it much easier to forgive what people have said or done to me personally than what they say or do to my children.

It is not unlike Corrie ten Boom's having to forgive the prison guard who was so cruel to her sister Betsie. Corrie saw this man viciously abuse her sister—who died shortly afterward—when both of them were in prison for protecting Jews in Holland during World War II. Years later, Corrie was seated on the platform of a church, preparing to speak in a service, when she spotted this very man in the audience. She struggled in her heart. She prayed in desperation for God to fill her heart with the love of Jesus. He did, but forgiveness became even more of a challenge when, after the service, this guard rather glibly said, in so many words, how good God is to forgive all of us. She wondered how sorry he was.[1]

It is often easier, then, it seems to me, to forgive what is done to us personally than what is done to those we love. But it is still very hard to forgive those who have hurt us directly, especially when they do not feel the slightest twinge of conscience. If our offender would put on sackcloth and ashes as a show of repentance, it would be much easier to forgive them.

But remember, at the foot of Jesus's cross no one seemed very sorry. There was no justice at His "trial"—if you could even call it that. A perverse glee filled the faces of the people who demanded His death: "'Crucify him!' they shouted" (Mark 15:13). Furthermore, "those who passed by hurled insults at him, shaking their heads and saying, 'So! You who are going to destroy the temple and build it in three days, come down from the cross and save yourself!'" (Mark 15:29–30). They shouted, "Let this Christ, this King of Israel, come down now from the cross, that we may see and believe" (Mark 15:32).

What was Jesus's response? "Father, forgive them, for they do not know what they are doing" (Luke 23:34). This must be our response as well.

Jesus could have said, "I forgive you." But such words might have been misinterpreted and wasted, like casting His pearls before swine. (See Matthew 7:6.) Instead Jesus asked the *Father* to forgive them, a far more grand gesture. Asking the Father to forgive them showed that not only had He forgiven them and released them from their guilt, but also that He had asked His Father not to punish or take revenge on them. It was not a perfunctory prayer; Jesus meant it. And it was gloriously answered! These offenders were among the very ones Peter addressed on the Day of Pentecost and who were converted. (See Acts 2:14–41.)

The Ultimate Proof of Total Forgiveness

The ultimate proof of total forgiveness takes place when we sincerely petition the Father to let those who have hurt us off the hook—even if they have hurt not only us, but also those close to us.

At the height of one of the fiercest eras at Westminster Chapel in the 1980s, I had to come face-to-face with this reality. I recalled Josif Tson's words to me, so I prayed for certain people to be forgiven. But I felt nothing; I just said the words.

"The ultimate proof of total forgiveness takes place when we sincerely petition the Father to let those who have hurt us off the hook—even if they have hurt not only us, but also those close to us."

However, after a few moments, it was as if the Lord said to me, "Do you know what you are asking Me to do?"

I thought I knew the answer to His question, so I said, "Yes."

He then seemed to reply, "Are you now asking Me to set them free as if they had done nothing wrong?"

That sobered me! I needed some time to think, but while I pondered His words, the Lord reminded me of the many sins for which He had forgiven *me*. I became frightened of the possibility that He might reveal—or let come out—some of the terrible things I had done.

I then humbly prayed, "Yes, Lord, I ask You to forgive them."

He then asked, "Do you mean that I should bless and prosper them?"

Once more I needed a little time. Then the Lord seemed to say, "What if I forgive and bless *you*, RT, in proportion to how you want Me to forgive and bless *them*?"

By this time I was boxed into a corner, and I surrendered. I began to sincerely pray for them to be forgiven and blessed as though they had caused me no offense. But I cannot truly say that my prayer was particularly godly or unselfish.

Some time ago there was a television series depicting Christians who had forgiven those who had hurt them. The producer, who was not a Christian, was profoundly moved. He said that while he could take or leave a church sermon, he could not ignore this. "Something must be happening in their lives," he said. It is so "unnatural" for a person to forgive those who hurt them and to desire reconciliation that there is no greater testimony to the lost.

This is, after all, the message of the New Testament: "That God was reconciling the world to himself in Christ, not counting men's sins against them. And he has committed to us the message of reconciliation" (2 Cor. 5:19). "But God demonstrates his own love for us in this: While we were still sinners, Christ died for us" (Rom. 5:8).

Once, while addressing a group of missionaries in the south of France, I stayed in the home of a Christian missionary who had been a Muslim. I was astonished at this change of life and marveled at his conversion. He told me that he had been led to Christ by some British soldiers when he lived in Madagascar. But what I really wanted to know was what had actually won him over to Christianity.

"What argument did they use?" I asked. "What line of reasoning persuaded you to turn from Islam to the Christian faith?"

> "What impresses the world most is *changed lives for which there is no natural explanation.*"

He replied, "It wasn't what they said; it was *who they were.*"

His statement really challenged me. It made me see the folly of imagining we are going to win people over by our superior arguments—or our great preaching methods. What impresses the world most is *changed lives for which there is no natural explanation.*

The Motivation to Forgive Can Have a Natural Explanation

The television producer of the show that focused on Christian forgiveness called such reconciliation "unnatural," but that is not quite true. The motivation to forgive often has a natural explanation, for Jesus speaks to us in a way that gets our attention—if only by appealing to our self-interest: "Do not judge, or you too will be judged" (Matt. 7:1). One selfish motive for not judging others is to keep from being judged ourselves.

If a person's chief desire is for a greater anointing, and he is told that this anointing will come in proportion to the degree that he forgives others, he will be more motivated to forgive. I, for one, want a greater anointing. If you could have seen my deepest heart when Josif Tson counseled me with the words, "You must totally forgive them," you might have discovered that I acquiesced because I wanted a greater blessing from God. So it is not entirely "unnatural" when one tries to forgive.

One Sunday I unexpectedly saw a person in one of our services who had seriously hurt one of our children. I noticed them just before I was scheduled to preach, and I felt as Corrie ten Boom must have felt when she spotted her prison guard in the audience. In a flash the Lord seemed to say to me, "You say you want to see a revival take place in this church. But what if the beginning of a mighty revival hinges on whether or not you totally forgive this person?"

I felt awful. I felt selfish. I felt trapped. But I had to make a decision on the spot as to whether or not I really wanted a revival in my church. I had to choose which meant more to me—getting even with someone who had hurt one of my children or receiving the blessing of the Spirit. I opted for the latter, but my prayer still had a natural explanation. I did not want it on my conscience that I had held up the blessing of the Spirit when all around me other believers were earnestly praying for it.

I still struggle in this area, but I believe that maybe—just maybe—I have totally forgiven this person. I have asked the Lord to bless them and even to let them off the hook. But it hasn't been easy. Totally forgiving someone doesn't necessarily mean we will want to spend our vacation with them, but it does mean that we release the bitterness in our hearts concerning what they have done.

Our Mandate Is to Forgive

God has given us a mandate regarding forgiveness in His Word:

> Be kind and compassionate to one another, forgiving each other, just as in Christ God forgave you.
>
> —EPHESIANS 4:32

> Bear with each other and forgive whatever grievances you may have against one another. Forgive as the Lord forgave you.
>
> —COLOSSIANS 3:13

> "Totally forgiving someone doesn't necessarily mean we will want to spend our vacation with them, but it does mean that we release the bitterness in our hearts concerning what they have done."

How has the Lord forgiven me? Unequivocally and unconditionally. My sins, which are many, will never be held against me, and nobody will even know what I did. "As far as the east is from the west, so far has he removed our transgressions from us" (Ps. 103:12). It therefore follows that I should not hold people responsible for what they have done to me. I will hold nothing against them, and I will not tell other people, not even my closest friends, what they did to me.

You might reply, "But you shared everything that had been done to you with Josif Tson." That's true. And I'm so glad I did! But I wasn't being malicious; I wasn't planning to start a smear campaign against anyone. Granted, my attitude was not perfect—I was seeking sympathy, but mercifully I was corrected. Without Josif's confrontation, I am not sure how long I could have kept silent. I can only thank God that He sent this wise person to me before I destroyed myself and my ministry.

David must have felt like this. In those years before he was made king—when he was "tomorrow's man" in a time of preparation—he was fully ready to take vengeance on Nabal, a man who had refused to help him in his time of need. But God sent Abigail—just in the nick of time—to appeal to David's common sense:

> David said to Abigail, "Praise be to the LORD, the God of Israel, who has sent you today to meet me. May you be blessed for your good judgment and for keeping me from bloodshed this day and from avenging myself with my own hands. Otherwise, as surely as the LORD, the God of Israel, lives, who has kept me from harming you, if you had not come quickly to meet me, not one male belonging to Nabal would have been left alive by daybreak."
>
> —1 SAMUEL 25:32–34

If you must tell another person what happened—because you can't contain the pain—tell only one, and choose someone who won't repeat it. I only hope they will be as faithful to you as Josif was to me.

When We Should Speak of the Grievance

"But what about the rapist?" you may ask. "Or the child abuser? Shouldn't the authorities be told?"

Can a person totally forgive and yet at the same time be the one who reports a crime? Absolutely. Total forgiveness does not mean closing our eyes to those who will continue to harm others. The apostle Paul ordered that the incestuous man in Corinth be put out of the church lest the entire church become corrupted. (See 1 Corinthians 5:5.) The rapist should be apprehended. The child abuser should be reported to the police, or he will continue to cause damage.

The types of offenses I primarily deal with in this book do not pertain to crimes that have been committed or scandalous sins that bedevil the church. Most of us do not encounter those situations on a day-to-day basis. Instead, I will address the small offenses that occur in daily life—the ones most Christians struggle to overcome; the ones that tempt us to harbor grudges and dream of revenge.

> "Total forgiveness does not mean closing our eyes to those who will continue to harm others."

There is admittedly a very thin line between the desire to see a rapist or child abuser punished because they are a danger to society and wanting them put in prison because they have hurt us or someone we love. The actual victim of the abuse is in a particular quandary. When we are personally offended, we usually disqualify ourselves from being the one to remove the speck from another's eye. (See Matthew 7:5.) But a person who has been raped must be a witness in a courtroom while simultaneously forgiving the offender. This is not easy!

What Total Forgiveness Is Not

Before going any further, let me clarify what total forgiveness is not—and then discuss what it is.

1. Approval of what they did

God never approved of our sin. He hates sin. In the Garden of Eden, He became angry with our first parents, Adam and Eve, because of their sin, but He still made garments of skin for them and clothed them (Gen. 3:21). This act of mercy demonstrated His forgiveness, even at that time. The garments of skin signified the sacrifice of blood that would be shed by the Redeemer who was to come.

In the New Testament, Jesus forgave the woman found in adultery, but He did not approve of what she did. He told her, "Leave your life of sin" (John 8:11).

So God did not approve of sin in biblical times—nor does He approve of sin today. We are to maintain a healthy respect and fear of God's justice and forgiveness: "But with you there is forgiveness; therefore you are feared" (Ps. 130:4).

Just as God forgives people without approving of their sin, we also must learn that forgiving people does not imply an endorsement of their evil deeds. We can forgive what we don't approve of because that is the way God has dealt with each of us.

2. Excusing what they did

We do not cover for the sins of other people. We do not point to circumstances in an attempt to explain away their behavior. While it is true that "every person is worth understanding," as Dr. Clyde Narramore says, this does not include excusing their inappropriate behavior.

> "Just as God forgives people without approving of their sin, we also must learn that forgiving people does not imply an endorsement of their evil deeds."

As Moses led the children of Israel across the desert toward the Promised Land, he was continually aggravated by their complaining. Eventually, after he had cried out to the Lord about the problem, he was offered a "new deal." God essentially said to him, "You have a sorry lot of people to lead, and they aren't following you very well. They have been stubborn and unteachable. I have decided to wipe them off the face of the earth and to start all over again with a new nation." (See Numbers 14:11–12.) Moses rejected God's offer and interceded for the people. In his prayer he did not excuse their behavior; instead, he appealed to God's mercy: "In accordance with your great love, forgive the sin of these people, just as you have pardoned them from the time they left Egypt until now" (Num. 14:19). And God forgave them.

3. Justifying what they did

To *justify* means to "make right or just." The *Oxford English Dictionary* says it means "to show (a person or statement or act, etc.) to be right or just or reasonable." There is no way that evil can be justified. God will never call something that is evil "right," and He does not require us to do so.

In Moses's prayer for the Israelite people, he did not offer a hint of justification for their behavior. Instead he pointed out to God that the Egyptians would not think very highly of God's power or name if they saw Him obliterate His own people. While we are required to forgive, we should never attempt to make what is wrong look like it is right.

4. Pardoning what they did

A pardon is a legal transaction that releases an offender from the consequences of their action, such as a penalty or a sentence. This is why we do not ask that the guilty rapist be exempt from punishment. He needs to pay his debt to society, and society must be protected from him.

I know of a lady who was raped by a person from a Middle Eastern country. At the time of the rape, she did not know he was from overseas; she found this out after he was caught. In the meantime she became a Christian. The police wanted her to testify at his trial. She was told he could be sent back to his homeland, which would mean he could be executed (the legal penalty for rape in his country).

She turned to me for advice. I counseled her to testify against this man. She had already forgiven him, but though she did not want to get him into trouble, if she did not testify, he would likely do it again. By the time she took the witness stand, there was no bitterness left in her heart; she was able to merely describe what had happened. As a result, the man was sent back to his own country. We never heard what happened to the man after he was extradited, but the potential punishment that he faced did not have any bearing on the forgiveness that had been offered by his victim.

5. Reconciliation

Forgiveness and reconciliation are not always the same. Reconciliation requires the participation of two people. The person you forgive may not want to see or talk to you. Or they may have passed away since the time of the offense. Moreover, you may not want to maintain a close relationship with the person you forgive.

Reconciliation implies a restoration of friendship after a quarrel. When a husband and wife totally forgive each other, it will usually mean a reconciliation—but not always. The bitterness and the desire to punish the other person may be gone, but the wish to restore things to the way they were may not necessarily be so strong. If your spouse is unfaithful and sleeps with your best friend, both your marriage and your friendship will probably never be the same, no matter how genuine the forgiveness that is offered.

An injured person can forgive an offender without reconciliation. It is wonderful indeed if the relationship can be restored, but this must not be pressed in most cases. Some things can never be the same again. It takes two to reconcile, and there must be a total willingness on both parts.

> Reconciliation requires the participation of two people.

As 2 Corinthians 5:19 tells us, God was in Christ, reconciling the world to Himself. But we still implore people on Christ's behalf: "Be reconciled to God" (v. 20). Why must we do this? Reconciliation doesn't really take place until both parties agree.

6. Denying what they did

Denying that an offense took place, or repression (suppressing what we really feel inside), is almost always unconscious. Some people, for various reasons, live in denial; that is, they refuse to admit or come to terms with the reality of a bad situation. It is sometimes painful to face the facts, and at times denial seems to be an easy way out.

Repression almost always has negative consequences for our psychological well-being. We often do it involuntarily, because, in some situations, the pain is too great to deal with on a conscious level. But repression cannot remove the wound. Even when the pain is pushed down into the cellar of our subconscious mind, it will still come out one way or another, often causing high blood pressure, nervousness, irritability, or even a heart attack.

Many victims of child abuse repress the memory of the event. The conscious mind cannot accept that a parent, a trusted friend, or a relative would do such a thing, so the victim often lives in denial. Rape victims experience the same phenomenon.

Total forgiveness is not carried out by repressing the offensive event. True forgiveness can only be offered after we have come to terms with reality—when we can admit, "This person actually did or said this to me."

7. Blindness to what happened

Some people, especially those with an "overly scrupulous conscience" (as some Puritans may call it), feel that to forgive is to be willfully and consciously blind to the sin that was committed. They feel that if they offer forgiveness, they are turning a blind eye to, or ignoring, the offense, and they believe that this would, in effect, be excusing a sin against God.

Willful blindness is slightly different from repression. Blindness is a conscious choice to pretend that a sin did not take place; repression is usually unconscious and involuntary.

Both are wrong and can be psychologically damaging. When we play such word games with ourselves, we can delay coming to terms with our own responsibility to forgive. Someone who is trying to forgive an offense but is actually pretending that the event never happened will eventually explode and become an offender themselves—all because they were not being true to the pain the original offense had caused.

Paul said that love "keeps no record of wrongs" (1 Cor. 13:5). But he did not mean that you must be blind to those wrongs. True forgiveness of a wrong does not pretend that no wrong is there. The Greek word used in this verse is *logizomai*, which means "to reckon or impute." Paul essentially is saying that "love does not store a wrong," that is, the wrong that was committed against us doesn't go into our "mental computer" to be reckoned with later. But the fact that there *is* something wrong, especially if it is staring you in the face, is not to be denied. In fact, the Greek word translated "wrong" in this verse is *kakon*, which means "evil." Because it is evil, it must be acknowledged. We cannot be blind to it. We should not pretend it didn't happen. That is not what total forgiveness means.

Sometimes if the person who hurt or wounded us is an authority figure or perhaps known to be very "godly," we may say to ourselves, "I didn't see this. I didn't hear this. This could not have happened; therefore, it didn't." But the truth is, sometimes the people we admire the most can do the most hurtful things to us. And it is of no value to pretend we didn't see it happen.

8. Forgetting

When someone says we must "forgive and forget," I understand what is meant. They are equating true forgiveness with wiping the memory of the event from their minds. But literally to forget may not be realistic. It is usually impossible to forget meaningful events in our lives, whether positive or negative. Sometimes deep trauma may cause amnesia of the event, but that is not a healthy form of forgetfulness. Often the way back to sanity after experiencing this type of amnesia is to try to remember everything—in detail.

Love doesn't erase our memories. It is actually a demonstration of greater grace when we are fully aware of what occurred—and we still choose to forgive. God doesn't literally forget our sins. He *chooses* to overlook them. He knows full well what we have done—every sordid detail. But He chooses not to remember so as to not hold our sins against us. (See Hebrews 8:12.) That is precisely what we are to do; although we may not be able to forget, we can still choose not to remember.

> "It is a demonstration of greater grace when we are fully aware of what occurred—and we still choose to forgive."

Deep hurts may never be eradicated as though they never happened. The truth is, they did happen. But even if we cannot totally forget, we must not dwell on them.

9. Refusing to take the wrong seriously

We cannot truly forgive until we see clearly the offense we are forgiving and understand its seriousness.

Some people may think that in order to forgive they must dismiss a wrong or pass it off as inconsequential or insignificant. But that is only avoiding the problem, possibly trying to make forgiveness easier. The greater victory for the one who does the forgiving is to face up to the seriousness—even the wickedness—of what happened and still forgive.

This is what God does. There is no sin too great for God to forgive. But He knows exactly what it is we've done and what it is He is forgiving. He doesn't say, "Come now, My dear, that's not too bad. I can easily wash *this* sin away." No. He sent His Son to die for sin, and Christ's sacrificial death proves just how serious a problem sin is. God doesn't pass our sins off as inconsequential, yet He forgives. Totally.

10. Pretending we are not hurt

It is ridiculous to think that we should have to keep a stiff upper lip when we have been injured by a spouse's infidelity...or betrayed...or molested...or unjustly criticized.

God let David know how grieved He was over the king's sins of adultery and murder. God did not pretend not to be hurt. David was a man after God's own heart (1 Sam. 13:14), and yet God was ruthlessly impartial with David. He was very grieved indeed.

Jesus was obviously hurt when He was struck in the face by a high priest's official. He even asked the man, "Why did you strike me?" (John 18:23). After all, Jesus endured the cross and scorned, rather than denied, the shame (Heb. 12:2). And He was able to say, "Father, forgive them, for they do not know what they are doing" (Luke 23:34).

What Total Forgiveness Is

Now let's take a look at what total forgiveness is.

1. Being aware of what someone has done and still forgiving them

As we saw above, total forgiveness is not being oblivious to what an offender did; it is not covering up, excusing, or refusing to acknowledge what happened. That would be living in denial. Some people choose to live in denial as a way of dealing with pain; this often happens during the time of grief when a loved one dies. But sooner or later the grieving person must come to terms with reality. As I said before, repression is almost never a good thing.

It is no spiritual victory to think we are forgiving people when we are only avoiding facing up to their wrong behavior. It is, if anything, evading true forgiveness. It is as though we are saying to ourselves, "I want to forgive them, but I don't think I really could if they actually did what it seems they did." So we postpone recognizing the true offense in order to keep from experiencing the pain, and we let them carry on as though nothing happened.

Total forgiveness is achieved only when we acknowledge what was done without any denial or covering up—and still refuse to make the offender pay for their crime. Total forgiveness is painful. It hurts when we kiss revenge good-bye. It hurts to think that the person is getting away with what they did and nobody else will ever find out. But when we know fully what they did and accept in our hearts that they will be blessed without any consequences for their wrong, we cross over into a supernatural realm. We begin to be a little more like Jesus, to change into the image of Christ.

2. Choosing to keep no record of wrongs

Love "keeps no record of wrongs" (1 Cor. 13:5). Why do we keep track of the times we are offended? To use them. To prove what happened. To wave them before someone who doubts what actually happened.

A husband may say to his wife in a moment of anger, "I'll remember that." And he does! She may say to him, "I will never forget this." And she doesn't!

> "Total forgiveness is a choice. It is not a feeling—at least at first—but is rather an act of the will."

Many marriages could be healed overnight if *both* parties would stop pointing the finger. Blaming others has been a common problem throughout human history, but God blesses the one who does away with the pointing of the finger. (See Isaiah 58:9.)

Love is a choice. Total forgiveness is a choice. It is not a feeling—at least at first—but is rather an act of the will. It is the choice to tear up the record of wrongs we have been keeping. We clearly see and acknowledge the evil that was done to us, but we erase it—or destroy the record—before it becomes lodged in our hearts. This way resentment does not have a chance to grow. When we develop a lifestyle of total forgiveness, we learn to erase the wrong rather than file it away in our mental computer. When we do this all the time—as a lifestyle—we not only avoid bitterness, but we also eventually experience total forgiveness as a feeling—and it is a good feeling.

3. Refusing to punish

Refusing to punish those who deserve it—giving up the natural desire to see them "get what's coming to them"—is the essence of total forgiveness. Our human nature cannot bear the thought that someone who hurt us deeply would get away with what they have done. It seems so unfair! We want vengeance—namely, their just punishment. But the fear that they won't get punished is the opposite of perfect love. This is why John said:

> There is no fear in love. But perfect love drives out fear, because fear has to do with *punishment*. The one who fears is not made perfect in love.
>
> —1 JOHN 4:18, EMPHASIS ADDED

If we harbor the desire to see our enemies punished, we will eventually lose the anointing of the Spirit. But when perfect love—the love of Jesus and the fruit of the Holy Spirit—enters, the desire for our enemy to be punished leaves. Total forgiveness is refusing to punish. It is refusing to cave in to the fear that this person or those people won't get their comeuppance—the punishment or rebuke we think they deserve.

I have been intrigued by John's assertion that fear "has to do with punishment." Sometimes we fear that God won't step in and give our enemies their just desserts. But if one gives in to this fear, he will be trespassing on God's territory, and God doesn't like that. Vindication is God's prerogative and God's prerogative alone. Deuteronomy 32:35 tells us, "It is mine to avenge; I will repay." This verse is even cited twice in the New Testament (Rom. 12:19; Heb. 10:30). Vindication is what God does best. He doesn't want our help. So when we refuse to be instruments of punishment, God likes that; it sets Him free to decide what should be done. But if we maneuver our way into the process, He may well let us do what we will; then neither divine vengeance nor true justice will be carried out—only the fulfillment of our personal grudge.

It is important that we examine ourselves in this area. We must ask, "How much of what I am about to say or do is just an attempt to punish?" If punishment is our motive, we are about to grieve the Holy Spirit, however much right may be on our side.

4. Not telling what they did

There is often a need to talk to someone about how you have been hurt, and this can be therapeutic if it is done with the right heart attitude. If this is necessary, you should choose the person you tell very carefully, making sure that person is trustworthy and will never repeat your situation to those it does not concern.

Anyone who truly forgives, however, does not gossip about his or her offender. Talking about how you have been wounded with the purpose of hurting your enemy's reputation or credibility is just a form of punishing them. Most of us do not talk about what happened for therapeutic reasons, but rather to keep our enemy from being admired. We divulge what that person did so others will think less of them. That is an attempt to punish—which is usurping God's arena of action.

When I recall that total forgiveness is forgiving others as I have been forgiven, I remember:

1. I won't be punished for my sins.
2. Nobody will know about my sins, for all sins that are under the blood of Christ will not be exposed or held against me.

Therefore when I blurt out what someone else has done to me, I am apparently forgetting that God will not tell what I did to Him. He has forgiven me of much, and He won't tell anyone about it. So, when I tell on my enemy, I am showing contempt for my own forgiveness.

I know that I have said that for therapeutic reasons we may share with another person the wrong that we have suffered. I believe that my conversation with Josif Tson falls into that category. There is no doubt that that encounter has caused things to work together for good for me (Rom. 8:28). And yet the funny thing is, had I the light and knowledge I now have on this subject,

I might never have told Josif in the first place. If you share your pain and offenses with someone else, examine your motives and be sure you aren't doing it to punish anyone by making them look bad. As Iago said in William Shakespeare's *Othello*:

> Who steals my purse steals trash; 'tis something, nothing;
> 'Twas mine, 'tis his, and has been slave to thousands;
> But he that filches from me my good name
> Robs me of that which not enriches him,
> And makes me poor indeed.[2]

5. Being merciful

"Blessed are the merciful, for they will be shown mercy" (Matt. 5:7). The Bible says basically two things about God:

- He is merciful.
- He is just.

The heart of the gospel is related to these two characteristics. Because He is merciful, God does not want to punish us; because He is just, He must punish us because we have sinned against Him. So how can both of these sides of God be satisfied simultaneously?

The answer is the crux of the gospel message: He sent His Son, Jesus Christ—the God-man—to die on the cross for us. "We all, like sheep, have gone astray, each of us has turned to his own way; and the LORD has laid on him the iniquity of us all" (Isa. 53:6). Because God punished Jesus for our sins, He can now be true to Himself and still be truly merciful to us.

> “Carrying out punishment also belongs to God alone.”

When we are told to be godly—which means to be like God—it does not follow that we can be like Him in every sense. After all, God is omnipotent (all-powerful), and we are not commanded to be that. He is omnipresent (present everywhere), and we can never do that. Carrying out punishment also belongs to God alone.

When it comes to being merciful, this is our Lord’s command: “Be merciful, just as your Father is merciful” (Luke 6:36). In the Greek language, mercy is the opposite of wrath or justice. One difference between grace and mercy is that grace is getting what we *don’t* deserve (favor), and mercy is not getting what we *do* deserve (justice). So when we show mercy, we are withholding justice from those who have injured us, and that is one aspect of godliness.

There is a fringe benefit for those of us who show mercy: we will also be shown mercy (Matt. 5:7). This again shows that total forgiveness is not devoid of self-interest. “The merciful man doeth good to his own soul” (Prov. 11:17, KJV).

6. Graciousness

True forgiveness shows grace and mercy at the same time. There is an interesting Greek word, *epieikes*, that means “forbearance” or “tolerance.” It comes from a root word that means the opposite of being unduly rigorous. In Hellenistic literature, Aristotle contrasted it with severely judging. The idea was: do not make a rigorous stand against your enemy even when you are clearly in the right.

> "Graciousness is shown by what you *don't* say, even if what you could say would be true."

In Philippians 4:5 this word is translated "gentleness." It comes down to our English word *graciousness*. It implies an exceedingly rare act of grace. It cuts right across a legalistic spirit, which is what comes naturally to most of us. This concept is quite threatening to those of us who don't suffer fools gladly, who feel that being inflexible for the truth is the ultimate virtue. Paul used this word in the context of a family squabble in Philippi: "I plead with Euodia and I plead with Syntyche to agree with each other in the Lord" (Phil. 4:2). If only each of them had been gracious. Both had strong personalities, and each probably had a following; each side was sure that they were right, and each wanted the other to look bad. "Try graciousness," says Paul. It is an unusual virtue.

Gracious is a word that described Jesus all the time. When a group of self-righteous religious leaders led a woman to Jesus who was found in the act of adultery, there was no question that sin had taken place. But what was our Lord's attitude? Graciousness. They wanted to see if He would throw the book at her.

> When they kept on questioning him, he straightened up and said to them, "If any one of you is without sin, let him be the first to throw a stone at her."
>
> —John 8:7

After the accusers slipped away:

> Jesus straightened up and asked her, "Woman, where are they? Has no one condemned you?"
>
> "No one, sir," she said.
>
> "Then neither do I condemn you," Jesus declared. "Go now and leave your life of sin."
>
> —JOHN 8:10–11

In this case there was no question a sin had taken place. But our Lord's attitude was to be gracious.

Graciousness is not the way presidential elections are won. A former presidential campaign manager claimed two facts:

- Candidates with high negative ratings in the opinion polls—above 35 percent—lose.
- Negative ratings are far easier to create than positive ones.

In other words, to win it is not enough to look good; you must also make your opponent look bad. And unfortunately it works.

But graciousness is withholding certain facts you know to be true, so as to leave your enemy's reputation unscathed. Graciousness is shown by what you *don't* say, even if what you could say would be true. Self-righteous people find it almost impossible to be gracious; they claim always to be after "the truth," no matter the cost. Total forgiveness sometimes means overlooking what you perceive to be the truth and not letting on about anything that could damage another person.

7. It is an inner condition.

Total forgiveness must take place in the heart or it is worthless, for "out of the overflow of the heart the mouth speaks" (Matt. 12:34). If we have not truly forgiven those who hurt us in our hearts, it will come out—sooner or later. But if it has indeed taken place in the heart, our words will show it. When there is bitterness, it will eventually manifest itself; when there is love, "there is nothing in him to make him stumble" (1 John 2:10).

This is why reconciliation is not essential for total forgiveness. If forgiveness truly takes place in the heart, one does not need to know whether one's enemy will reconcile. If I have forgiven him in my heart of hearts, but he still doesn't want to speak to me, I can still have the inner victory. It may be far easier to forgive when we know that those who maligned or betrayed us are sorry for what they did, but if I must have this knowledge before I can forgive, I may never have the victory over my bitterness.

> "Confidence toward God is ultimately what total forgiveness is all about; He is the One I want to please at the end of the day."

Those who believe that they are not required to forgive unless their offender has first repented are not following Jesus's example on the cross.

> Jesus said, "Father, forgive them, for they do not know what they are doing." And they divided up his clothes by casting lots.
>
> —LUKE 23:34

If Jesus had waited until His enemies felt some guilt or shame for their words and actions, He would never have forgiven them.

It is my experience that most people we must forgive do not believe they have done anything wrong at all, or if they know that they did something wrong, they believe it was justified. I would even go so far as to say that at least 90 percent of all the people I've ever had to forgive would be indignant at the thought that they had done something wrong. If you gave them a lie-detector test, they would honestly say that they had done nothing wrong—and they would pass the test with flying colors.

Total forgiveness, therefore, must take place in the heart. If I have a genuine heart experience, I will not be devastated if there is no reconciliation. If those who hurt me don't want to continue a relationship with me, it isn't my problem, because I have forgiven them. This is also why a person can achieve inner peace even when forgiving someone who has died. The apostle John wrote, "Dear friends, if our *hearts* do not condemn us, we have confidence before God" (1 John 3:21, emphasis added). Confidence toward God is ultimately what total forgiveness is all about; He is the One I want to please at the end of the day. He cares and knows whether I have truly and totally forgiven, and when I *know* I have His love and approval, I am one very happy and contented servant of Christ.

8. It is the absence of bitterness.

Bitterness is an inward condition. It is an excessive desire for vengeance that comes from deep resentment. It heads the list of the things that grieve the Spirit of God. (See Ephesians 4:30ff.) It became Esau's preoccupation. (See Genesis 27:41.) And it is one of the most frequent causes of people missing the grace of God. "See to it that no one misses the grace of God and that no bitter root grows up to cause trouble and defile many" (Heb. 12:15). Bitterness will manifest itself in many ways—losing your temper, high blood pressure, irritability, sleeplessness, obsession with getting even, depression, isolation, a constant negative perspective, and generally feeling unwell.

We must, therefore, begin to get rid of a bitter and unforgiving spirit; otherwise, the attempt to forgive will fail. It is true that doing the right things, even when you don't feel like it, can eventually lead to having the right feelings. But the very act of trying to do right shows that the bitterness is not as deep as it could be. In other words, if someone feels bitter but begins to put the principle of total forgiveness into action, it shows that he or she is not totally controlled by bitterness. Otherwise he or she wouldn't make a start in doing what is right.

The absence of bitterness allows the Holy Spirit to be Himself in us. This means that I will become like Jesus. When the Spirit is grieved, I am left to myself, and I will struggle with emotions ranging from anger to fear. But when the Holy Spirit is not grieved, He is *at home* with me; He will begin to change me into the person He wants me to be, and I will be able to manifest the gentleness of the Spirit. Relinquishing bitterness is an open invitation for the Holy Spirit to give you His peace, His joy, and the knowledge of His will.

This is extremely important when it comes to the matter of reconciliation. Let's say, for example, your best friend has had an affair with your wife. Must you forgive him? Yes. But it does not follow that you will remain closest of friends. If I have totally forgiven the person who has hurt me and I have no bitterness, I should not feel the slightest bit of guilt or shame for not wanting a complete restoration of that relationship. Even if there never had been a friendship in the first place, if someone has greatly wronged me, I can forgive him and yet see it as totally reasonable not to invite him to lunch every Sunday.

"Relinquishing bitterness is an open invitation for the Holy Spirit to give you His peace, His joy, and the knowledge of His will."

The essential factor is that there is no trace of bitterness. How can we be sure that there is no bitterness left in our hearts? Bitterness is gone when there is no desire to get even with or punish the offender, when I do or say nothing that would hurt his reputation or future, and when I truly wish him well in all he seeks to do.

9. Forgiving God

Although we often do not see it at first—and for some it takes a long time—all of our bitterness is ultimately traceable to a resentment of God. This may be an unconscious anger. Some "good" people would be horrified at the thought that they could be harboring bitterness toward God. But we often repress this, too; such knowledge is too painful to admit.

The truth is, our bitterness is often aimed at God. Why do we feel this way? Because deep in our hearts we believe that He is the one who allowed bad things to happen in our lives. Since He is all-powerful and all-knowing, couldn't He have prevented tragedies and offenses from happening? He has allowed us to suffer when we didn't do anything, or so it seems, to warrant such ill treatment. What we ultimately believe is that God is to blame for our hurt.

Only a fool would claim to know the full answer to the question: Why does God allow evil and suffering to continue when He has the power to stop it? But there is a partial answer: He does so in order that we may believe. There would be no need for faith if we knew the answer concerning the origin of evil and the reason for suffering. I only know that it is what makes faith possible.

I know something else as well:

> All things work together for good to them that love God, to them who are the called according to his purpose.
>
> —Romans 8:28, KJV

> Although we often do not see it at first, all of our bitterness is ultimately traceable to a resentment of God.

God does turn evil into blessing. He causes things to work together for good. God did not send His Son into the world to explain evil, but rather to save us from it and to exemplify a life of suffering. Jesus, who was and is the God-man, suffered as no one else has or ever will. One day God will clear His own name from the charge of being unjust, but in the meantime, we need to trust Him and take Him at His Word that He is just and merciful.

As for all the unhappy things He has allowed to happen to me, I affirm His justice. He is God. He knows exactly what He is doing—and why. For all of us who struggle with God's right to allow evil to exist in the world, there still must be a genuine forgiveness on our part, for any bitterness toward God grieves the Holy Spirit. We therefore must forgive Him—though He is not guilty—for allowing evil to touch our lives.

If we will patiently wait for God's purposes to be fulfilled, at the end of the day—this is a guarantee—we will say that He has done all things well, even in what He permitted. He was never guilty in the first place, but because He sometimes appears to us to have been unfair, we must relinquish our bitterness and wholly forgive Him before we can move on with our lives.

10. Forgiving ourselves

Total forgiveness, then, means forgiving people—totally—and also forgiving God. But it also must include the total forgiveness of ourselves.

One common complaint every church leader hears is this: "I know God forgives me, but I just can't seem to forgive myself." This is such an important concept that we will discuss it further later in the book. But I must say here and now: there is no lasting joy in forgiveness if it doesn't include forgiving yourself. It is anything but *total* forgiveness if we forgive God and those who hurt us but we are unable to forgive ourselves. It is as wrong as not forgiving others, because God loves us just as much as He loves others; He will be just as unhappy when we don't forgive ourselves as when we hold a grudge against others. Put simply, we matter to God. He wants our lives to be filled with joy. He not only wants us to forgive ourselves, but He also wants it urgently.

Total forgiveness brings such joy and satisfaction that I am almost tempted to call it a selfish enterprise. As we have seen, the wider research that is taking place these days has already overwhelmingly concluded that the first person to experience delight when forgiveness takes place is the one who forgives.

> "There is no lasting joy in forgiveness if it doesn't include forgiving yourself."

I pray that what has been written and what follows will challenge and motivate you to forgive those who have hurt you, to forgive the God who let it happen, and to forgive yourself—totally.

Tears of despair and confusion gave way to the words, "I never believed it could happen to me." I was devastated, betrayed, and dazed. Head in hands, I was quickly sinking into hopelessness. Self-pity was giving way to a hurt and bitterness it seemed I was powerless to escape. Brother Kendall's book, *Total Forgiveness,* was the right word at the right time. The book did not provide a soft shoulder to cry on, but it did provide a Rock to stand on. Precept upon precept I was moved from self-pity and unforgiveness to layers of truth that refused to leave me as they found me. *Total Forgiveness* was no how-to manual on forgiving. It was for me a platform for the Word to transform my personal devastation to total forgiveness, through the supernatural gift of grace to forgive.

—*T.B.*

2

HOW TO KNOW WE HAVE TOTALLY FORGIVEN

Now hurry back to my father and say to him, "This is what your son Joseph says: God has made me lord of all Egypt. Come down to me; don't delay. You shall live in the region of Goshen and be near me—you, your children and grandchildren, your flocks and herds, and all you have. I will provide for you there, because five years of famine are still to come. Otherwise you and your household and all who belong to you will become destitute."

—*Genesis 45:9–11*

After my life was changed by taking Josif Tson's advice to heart, I began to teach this message of total forgiveness from place to place. But after my teaching, people began coming up to me with this question: "How do I know when I have totally forgiven someone?" They would sometimes say, "I think I have forgiven my offender, but I'm not sure."

The truth is, I didn't know how to answer them. I began to wonder whether I had totally forgiven certain people who had hurt me. The question bothered me so much that I began to search for an answer.

> "Joseph provides a heart-searching frame of reference by showing us how he was able to totally forgive his brothers."

I found it—unexpectedly. I began preaching about the life of Joseph in June 1982. I had invited Arthur Blessitt, the man who has carried the cross around the world and who holds the record in the *Guinness Book of Records* for the world's longest walk, to preach for us at Westminster Chapel. His ministry turned our church upside down. We began to add worship songs to our services instead of singing just the old-fashioned hymns. We began our Pilot Light ministry, witnessing on the streets between Victoria and Buckingham Palace on Saturday mornings. And we started inviting people to come forward and confess Christ publicly after the Sunday evening services. The first Sunday night after Arthur Blessitt's visit, I delivered my first sermon on the life of Joseph, and my first appeal for people to accept Christ prompted seven people to come forward.

Joseph and Total Forgiveness

The account of Joseph's revealing his identity to his brothers is found in Genesis 45. And it is in these verses that I found my answer to the question, "How can I know whether I have truly forgiven someone?" Joseph provides a heart-searching frame of reference by showing us how he was able to totally forgive his brothers.

Twenty-two years earlier, Joseph's brothers had conspired to kill him because they were jealous of the attention he got from their father. As Jacob's favorite child, Joseph strutted around in a richly ornamented robe, a coat of many colors. In addition, Joseph dreamed that his eleven brothers would one day come begging to him, and showing no sensitivity or humility at all:

> He said to them, "Listen to this dream I had: We were binding sheaves of grain out in the field when suddenly my sheaf rose and stood upright, while your sheaves gathered around mine and bowed down to it."
>
> His brothers said to him, "Do you intend to reign over us? Will you actually rule us?" And they hated him all the more because of his dream and what he had said.
>
> Then he had another dream, and he told it to his brothers. "Listen," he said, "I had another dream, and this time the sun and moon and eleven stars were bowing down to me."
>
> —Genesis 37:6–9

It doesn't take Sigmund Freud to interpret those dreams! And yet the dreams were from God. There was nothing wrong with Joseph's gift—which had to do with the interpretation of dreams—but there was a lot wrong with Joseph. God's hand was on Joseph's life, but because this young man needed to learn temperance, God allowed Joseph's brothers to deal with him ruthlessly. Instead of killing him, they decided on plan B—selling him as a slave to the Ishmaelites. This they did, never expecting to see him again.

In order to explain Joseph's sudden absence to their father, the brothers concocted a clever cover-up. They dipped Joseph's robe in some goat's blood and then took it to Jacob. They deceived him, saying, "We found this. Examine it to see whether it is your son's robe" (Gen. 37:32). The plan worked.

> He [Jacob] recognized it and said, "It is my son's robe! Some ferocious animal has devoured him. Joseph has surely been torn to pieces."
>
> Then Jacob tore his clothes, put on sackcloth and mourned for his son many days. All his sons and daughters came to comfort him, but he refused to be comforted. "No," he said, "in mourning will I go down to the grave to my son." So his father wept for him.
>
> —Genesis 37:33–35

> "There was nothing wrong with Joseph's gift—which had to do with the interpretation of dreams—but there was a lot wrong with Joseph."

Even though the situation looked bleak, God was with Joseph. He began to work in the house of Potiphar, the Egyptian officer to whom the Ishmaelites had sold him. He was such a valuable employee that he was put in charge of the entire household. But the Bible describes Joseph as "well-built and handsome," and some time later Potiphar's wife began to flirt with him. "Come to bed with me!" she pleaded, but he refused.

As the saying goes, "Hell hath no fury like a woman scorned." After being rejected repeatedly, she decided to accuse Joseph of rape. Potiphar believed his wife and had Joseph put in prison. Joseph was punished for doing the right thing! But as Peter said, "It is commendable if a man bears up under the pain of unjust suffering because he is conscious of God. But how is it to your credit if you receive a beating for doing wrong and endure it? But if you suffer for doing good and you endure it, this is commendable before God" (1 Pet. 2:19–20).

This was the beginning of a period of preparation for Joseph. Joseph didn't realize it at the time, but God had great plans for him. Dr. Martyn Lloyd-Jones, my predecessor at Westminster Chapel, used to say to me, "The worst thing that can happen to a man is to succeed before he is ready." God wanted to ensure that Joseph did not come out of prison and embark on the next phase of his life's work until he was ready.

> The Lord disciplines those he loves, and he punishes everyone he accepts as a son.
>
> —Hebrews 12:6

Joseph had much to be bitter about. First, his brothers had treated him with cruelty and disdain. True, he had made them jealous and had not been a very nice guy—he had even been a tattletale. (See Genesis 37:2.) But killing him or selling him to the Ishmaelites was a wicked and evil act.

Second, Joseph had been falsely accused. Instead of sleeping with Potiphar's wife, he had resisted the temptation. We all like to think that God will bless us when we are faithful and obedient to His Word, but the thanks Joseph got was imprisonment.

Third, God allowed all of these things to take place. Joseph's rationale for resisting the overtures of Potiphar's wife was loyalty to God: "How then could I do such a wicked thing and sin against God?" he implored (Gen. 39:9). Many people I know are afraid to have an affair for only one reason—the fear of getting caught. But Joseph was in Egypt where nobody knew him—his family was faraway back in Canaan—and Potiphar's wife wasn't going to tell. Joseph was faithful because he didn't want to displease God. But then God allowed Joseph to go to prison for something he didn't even do.

> "If we are walking in love, we will not play the manipulator when it comes to promoting ourselves; we will let God promote us in His timing."

Joseph had much to be bitter about, then, and many "offenders" to forgive: his brothers who sold him into slavery, Potiphar's wife who lied, and God who let it all happen.

After some time passed, Joseph had company in prison—Pharaoh's cupbearer and baker. While there, each of them had a dream that Joseph offered to interpret. He predicted that the baker would be hanged in three days, but that the cupbearer would get his job back in the same span of time. Both of those events took place just as Joseph predicted. So far, so good.

But a temptation too great—so it seemed—was handed to Joseph on a silver platter. He had barely finished telling the cupbearer that he would be restored to Pharaoh's favor when Joseph got too involved in his prophetic word:

> But when all goes well with you, remember me and show me kindness; mention me to Pharaoh and get me out of this prison. For I was forcibly carried off from the land of the Hebrews, and even here I have done nothing to deserve being put in a dungeon.
>
> —Genesis 40:14–15

Most of us would have done the same thing. But God had special plans for Joseph, and in order for his testimony to be validated later, there could be no promotion that could be explained in terms of what a human being could do. In other words, God wanted Joseph out of prison as much as Joseph wanted to get out. But if the cupbearer simply put in a good word for Joseph—and he got sprung from prison because of it—it would have fallen far short of God's supreme plan. Delays can actually be part of God's purpose; seemingly unanswered prayer can be as much a part of God's will as answered prayer.

The truth is, Joseph needed to be delivered from bitterness and self-pity. First Corinthians 13:5, the same verse that says love "keeps no record of wrongs," also says that love "is not self-seeking." If we are walking in love, we will not play the manipulator when it comes to promoting ourselves; we will let God promote us in His timing. Joseph was full of self-pity. He says so: "I have done nothing to deserve being put in a dungeon" (Gen. 40:15). Self-pity and self-righteousness—twin sins that complement each other—are eclipsed when we begin to forgive totally and keep no record of wrongs. At that point in time, Joseph had not yet forgiven his brothers, Potiphar's wife, or God.

Joseph had not forgotten his dreams. He knew that one day—for one reason or another—his brothers would bow down before him. And eventually they did. But when it finally happened, Joseph was a changed man. There was no bitterness. There were no grudges. None. Something had happened to him during those final two years in prison. How do I know that? Look at him; listen to him! His attitude had completely changed. He had totally and wonderfully forgiven them all. Before his heart was changed, he probably fantasized about the day they would come begging him for forgiveness; he probably longed to see the fulfillment of his dreams, to say "Gotcha!" to his brothers, and then to throw the book at them. Instead, when the time came, he lovingly welcomed them and forgave them with tears.

> "The moment finally came when Joseph revealed himself. Filled with love, he demonstrated total forgiveness."

What caused such a dramatic change? Two years after Joseph had interpreted the dreams of the baker and the cupbearer, Pharaoh himself had a dream—two dreams in fact—and none of his magicians and astrologers could figure them out. The cupbearer overheard the commotion and remembered how Joseph had interpreted his dream so accurately. He stepped forward and recommended Joseph to Pharaoh. Suddenly Joseph found himself before the ruler of Egypt, and he alone was able to interpret the dreams: there would be seven years of plenty followed by seven years of famine in the land. Joseph also offered his advice: Pharaoh should store up food during the first seven years so that there would be a surplus available during the seven years of lack—not only for Egypt but also for the surrounding countries who would come to Egypt begging for food.

Pharaoh was so impressed with this wise advice that he made Joseph the prime minister of Egypt right on the spot! God did it all. He had used the cupbearer, yes, but not because of Joseph's manipulation.

Then, during the time of famine, who do you suppose came to Egypt begging for food? Joseph's brothers. He recognized them instantly, though they didn't know who he was—twenty-two years older and wearing official Egyptian garb, not to mention speaking Egyptian through an interpreter. The moment finally came when Joseph revealed himself. It was the moment he dreamed of. But instead of punishing them, which he had the power to do, he wept. Filled with love, he demonstrated total forgiveness.

Applying Joseph's Example to Ourselves

What lessons about total forgiveness can the example of Joseph teach us?

1. Do not let anyone know what someone said about you or did to you.

To ensure privacy, Joseph cried out, "Have everyone leave my presence!" (Gen. 45:1). He waited to reveal his identity until there was no one in the room except his brothers. Even the interpreter, who had no idea Joseph could speak Hebrew, was, to his surprise, told to leave.

But why? Why did Joseph make everyone else leave? Because he did not want a single person in Egypt to know what his brothers had done to him twenty-two years before. He had a plan: namely, to persuade them to bring their father, Jacob, to Egypt. He wanted his entire family there with him. No one in Egypt needed to know what they had done.

Joseph was a hero in Egypt. The people were in awe of him. By interpreting Pharaoh's dreams he had saved the nation. He knew that if the word leaked out that his brothers had actually kidnapped him and sold him to Ishmaelites, the Egyptians would hate his brothers. Instead, Joseph wanted them to be heroes in Egypt as he was, and the only way to cause that to happen was to ensure that absolutely nobody in Egypt would ever discover their wickedness. So he did not allow anyone to eavesdrop on this historic conversation as he revealed his identity to those startled, frightened men. Joseph not only did not let anybody know what they had done; he ensured that they *could* not know. That is one of the proofs that one has totally forgiven.

This is precisely how you and I are forgiven: "As far as the east is from the west, so far has he removed our transgressions from us" (Ps. 103:12). Our sins are "wiped out" (Acts 3:19). It is as though our sins don't exist anymore—they are gone, gone, gone, gone! Insofar as our standing and security with God are concerned, they will never be held against us. Back in the hills of Kentucky, we used to sing a chorus about our sins being buried in God's sea of forgetfulness. This is based on Micah 7:19: "You will again have compassion on us; you will tread our sins underfoot and hurl all our iniquities into the depths of the sea."

God will not reveal what He knows. Picture, if you will, a giant screen such as the ones many churches use for projecting the words to worship songs. Imagine your sins listed on that screen for people to see. You would look at the list and be forced to admit, "Yes—that's true. But I thought I was forgiven and that nobody would know!" Imagine the sense of betrayal you would feel if God disclosed to everyone else what He knows about you!

There are a lot of things God knows about me that I wouldn't want anyone else to know. He has enough on me to bury me! But you will never know any of it, because God won't tell.

> "It is as though our sins don't exist anymore—they are gone, gone, gone, gone!"

So why do we tell on other people? If for therapeutic reasons we tell one other person who will never repeat it, that is understandable. But the real reason we usually tell is to *punish.* And one weapon at our disposal to accomplish this is our tongue. We tell everyone else what we know in order to make our offender look bad! If we can hurt their credibility or reputation in return for their hurting us, "Good!" we say. "It serves them right." We blab to everyone we can find what was done to us as a way of getting even.

Joseph is sometimes referred to as a type of Christ—a person in the Old Testament who, long before Jesus came along, displayed characteristics of Jesus Himself. And despite his imperfections, Joseph was indeed a type of Christ in many ways. His ability to forgive his brothers as he did foreshadows Jesus's actions toward

His disciples. Scared to death and ashamed over the way they had deserted Jesus when He was arrested, they were huddled behind closed doors when the resurrected Jesus turned up unexpectedly and declared, "Peace be with you!" (John 20:21). The disciples were totally forgiven—and they knew it.

"It is comforting to know that God freely and totally forgives all of our sins and will never tell what He knows."

We all have skeletons in our closets; some are known to others; many are unknown. It is comforting to know that God freely and totally forgives all of our sins and will never tell what He knows. That is the way Joseph forgave. And that is why we are urged, "Be kind and compassionate to one another, forgiving each other, just as in Christ God forgave you" (Eph. 4:32).

2. Do not allow anyone to be afraid of you or intimidated by you.

Joseph revealed his identity to his brothers with tears and compassion. The last thing he wanted was for them to fear him. He had been aching to let them know who he was, but he was following a carefully thought-out strategy and wanted to be sure the plan would work. When he could "no longer control himself," he broke down and told them who he was. "And he wept so loudly that the Egyptians heard him, and Pharaoh's household heard about it" (Gen. 45:2).

Joseph's immediate concern was not only to reveal who he was to his brothers, but also to learn the condition of his father.

> Joseph said to his brothers, "I am Joseph! Is my father still living?" But his brothers were not able to answer him, because they were terrified at his presence.
>
> —Genesis 45:3

When we have not totally forgiven those who hurt us, it gives us a bit of pleasure to realize that they are afraid or intimidated. If someone who has hurt us—and knows it—freezes in anxiety when they see us approach, we may say to ourselves, "Good! They *should* be afraid of me!" But that only shows that there is still bitterness in our hearts. "Perfect love drives out fear, because fear has to do with punishment" (1 John 4:18). If people are afraid of us, we fancy they are getting a bit of punishment—which is what we want if we are not walking in forgiveness.

But this was not the pattern of Joseph's life. Knowing they were "terrified at his presence," he said to them, "Come close to me." Why did he direct them to do this? For two reasons: He did not want them to be afraid, and he longed to embrace every single one of them—which he later did.

Fear can cause us to do silly things. Our insecurity is what causes us to want people to stand in awe of us. We become pretentious; we try to keep other people from knowing who we really are and what we are really like. Sometimes I think the most attractive thing about Jesus as a man was His unpretentiousness. Jesus did not try to create an "aura of mystique"; even common people could relate to Him.

In terms of prestige and power, Joseph had ascended as high as one could. Had he so desired, he could have kept his brothers at a distance. He could have demanded that they praise him for his success; he could have made them fall at his feet in fear and reverence. He could have reminded them of his dreams and their disbelief. He could have even said one of the favorite phrases of human beings everywhere: "I told you so."

But, no. That is not what Joseph did. "Come close to me," he said. He did not feel a cut above them. He had no desire for them to stand back and say, "Wow! Look at our brother Joseph." He wanted them to feel no fear in his presence. He wanted to be loved rather than admired.

Paul said, "For you did not receive a spirit that makes you a slave again to fear, but you received the Spirit of sonship. And by him we cry, '*Abba*, Father'" (Rom. 8:15, emphasis added). The word *Abba* is a pure Aramaic word that is the equivalent of the word *Daddy*. The witness of the Holy Spirit makes us feel loved and accepted. Once He has forgiven us, God does not want us to be afraid of Him. This should not mean that we develop a cheap familiarity with Him, much less lose a sense of His glory and might, but He wants us to experience His fatherly tenderness.

What Joseph wanted his brothers to feel is what Jesus wants us to feel about Himself and the Father. "Anyone who has seen me has seen the Father," said Jesus (John 14:9). If you had an abusive or absentee father, you may understandably have trouble relating to God as a Father. But there is no law that says we have to have perfect fathers before we can rightly relate to our heavenly Father. The perfect image for us to follow can be found in Jesus Christ—and it is also what Joseph was trying to convey to his brothers.

Joseph did not require them to feel a trace of fear or show further how sorry they were before he forgave them; instead, he wanted them to love him and feel his love for them in return.

> "Once He has forgiven us, God does not want us to be afraid of Him."

This is the kind of relationship that Jesus desires with us. He wants to put us at ease in His presence. When Jesus met with the eleven disciples in the upper room after His resurrection, there was no hint of rebuke for their desertion and betrayal before His crucifixion. Jesus never said, "How could you have abandoned Me like that?" Instead, He picked up where He left off before the whole ordeal began and said, "As the Father has sent me, I am sending you" (John 20:21).

"There is no fear in love" (1 John 4:18). Joseph did not want his brothers to be afraid, and when we have totally forgiven our offenders, we will not want them to be afraid either.

3. We will want them to forgive themselves and not feel guilty.

When the eleven brothers had difficulty believing Joseph's revelation, he repeated it: "I am your brother Joseph, the one you sold into Egypt!" (Gen. 45:4). He had not forgotten what they had done, nor did he pretend that it hadn't happened; he was simply identifying himself to them.

Knowing exactly what they were thinking, he said, "And now, do not be distressed and do not be angry with yourselves for selling me here" (Gen. 45:5). He was not about to send them on a guilt trip; he knew that they felt guilty enough (Gen. 42:21).

> "Forgiveness is worthless to us emotionally if we can't forgive ourselves."

Sometimes we say, in effect, "I forgive you for what you did, but I hope you feel bad about it." This shows we still want to see them punished. It shows our own fear, which, I repeat, "has to do with punishment" (1 John 4:18). But when our fear is gone, the desire to see others punished goes with it.

We love to punish people by making them feel guilty. Those of us who are always sending people on guilt trips almost certainly have a big problem ourselves with a sense of guilt. Because we haven't sorted out our own guilt issues, we want to make sure others wallow in the mire of guilty feelings with us. We point the finger partly because we haven't forgiven ourselves.

I sometimes think guilt is one of the most painful feelings in the world. My own greatest pain over the years has been guilt—and being reminded of my own failure, especially as a parent. If someone wanted to hurt me—to really and truly make me feel awful—all they would have to do is ask, "How much time did you spend with your kids in those critical years as they were growing up?" I am grateful that my children have totally forgiven me for my sins as a parent, but I still struggle with feelings of guilt for the mistakes that I made.

Joseph wanted to set his brothers free. He did not want them to blame or be angry with themselves; he wanted them to forgive themselves. Forgiveness is worthless to us emotionally if we can't forgive ourselves. And it certainly isn't *total* forgiveness unless we forgive ourselves as well as others.

God knows this. This is why He wants us to forgive ourselves as well as to accept His promise that our past is under the blood of Christ. Joseph was trying to do what Jesus would do: make it easy for his brothers to forgive themselves.

To ease their minds, Joseph gave an explanation for his suffering: "It was to save lives that God sent me ahead of you" (Gen. 45:5). God does that with us as well; He wants to make it easy for us to forgive ourselves. That is partly why He gave us what is possibly Paul's most astonishing promise:

> And we know that all things work together for good to them that love God, to them who are the called according to his purpose.
>
> —Romans 8:28, kjv

God doesn't want us to continue to feel guilty, so He says, "Just wait and see. I will cause everything to work together for good to such an extent that you will be tempted to say that even the bad things that happened were good and right." Not that they were, of course, for the fact that all things work together for good doesn't mean necessarily that they were right at the time. But God has a way of making bad things *become* good.

This, then, is total forgiveness: not wanting our offenders to feel guilty or upset with themselves for what they did, and showing them that there is a reason God let it happen.

4. We will let them save face.

Allowing those who have offended us to save face is carrying the principle of total forgiveness a step further. Joseph told his brothers something that is, without doubt, the most magnanimous, gracious, and emancipating statement he had made so far: "You didn't do this to me; God did."

> But God sent me ahead of you to preserve for you a remnant on earth and to save your lives by a great deliverance. So then, it was not you who sent me here, but God. He made me father to Pharaoh, lord of his entire household and ruler of all Egypt.
>
> —Genesis 45:7–8

This is as good as it gets. When we can forgive like that, we're there. We have achieved total forgiveness.

Saving face. It is what God lets us do.

What exactly is "saving face"? Dale Carnegie uses this expression in his book *How to Win Friends and Influence People*.[1] Although this is not specifically a Christian book, it is saturated with Christian principles and would do most Christians no harm to read. Saving face means preserving one's dignity and self-esteem. It is not only the refusal to let a person feel guilty; it is providing a rationale that enables what they did to look good rather than bad. Or it may mean hiding a person's error from people so they can't be embarrassed.

> "Saving face. It is what God lets us do."

You can make a friend for life by letting someone save face. I gather this is an Oriental expression, because for an Oriental the worst thing on earth is to lose face. Some have been known to commit suicide rather than lose face. But I have a suspicion that, deep down, we are all the same when it comes to losing face—none of us want it to happen.

God lets us save face by causing our past (however foolish) to work out for our good. If you read the genealogy of Jesus in Matthew 1, you might think that the sin of adultery between David and Bathsheba was part of the divine strategy all along. I doubt that is the case. David's sin of adultery—and the attempted cover-up involving the murder of Uriah—must rank as one of the worst crimes in the history of God's people. But Matthew 1:6 records these events as though what happened was supposed to have happened in just that way.

Can you imagine the look on the faces of his brothers when Joseph said to them, "So then it was not you who sent me here, but God" (Gen. 45:8)? Reuben may have said to Judah, "Did we hear him correctly? Did he say that we didn't do what we did, but God did it instead?" To have believed a statement like that would have meant an unimaginable burden of guilt rolled off these men. It would have been news too good to be true.

How could this be? According to Joseph, the answer was simple: God predestined that Abraham's descendants would live in Egypt. He simply sent Joseph ahead of the rest of his family. In other words, Joseph was literally saying, "Somebody had to go first, and I was chosen. God knew about the famine and that our family, the family of Israel, had to be preserved."

There is more. By saying what he did, Joseph was also admitting that, if he had been in their shoes, he would have done what they did. He did not condemn them for what they did. He had reached an understanding of their actions.

For the one who totally forgives from the heart, there is little self-righteousness. Two reasons we are *able* to forgive are:

- We see what we ourselves have been forgiven of.
- We see what we are capable of.

When we are indignant over someone else's wickedness, there is the real possibility either that we are self-righteous or that we have no objectivity about ourselves. When we truly see ourselves as we are, we will recognize that we are just as capable of committing any sin as anyone else. We are saved only by God's intervening grace.

This was no self-righteous man reaching out to his brothers. Joseph was not being condescending or patronizing, nor was he consciously performing some great feat. He was not thinking, "I will be admired for being so gracious to these unworthy, evil men." Quite the contrary; Joseph had already forgiven his brothers during those two years in the dungeon when God operated on his heart. He became a trophy of sovereign grace, an example of forgiveness for us to follow.

"When we truly see ourselves as we are, we will recognize that we are just as capable of committing any sin as anyone else."

Letting his brothers save face, then, was not simply a polite gesture; Joseph was telling his brothers the truth. God *had* meant it for good; God *did* send Joseph to Egypt with a purpose in mind. Joseph was not one whit better than a single one of them, and he was not about to act like it. He simply felt grateful to see them again and grateful to God for everything that he had been brought through. The preparation, the false accusations, all of the lies, pain, and suffering were worth it.

It is reminiscent of Jesus's words to His disciples: "A woman giving birth to a child has pain because her time has come; but when her baby is born she forgets the anguish because of her joy that a child is born into the world. So with you: Now is your time of grief, but I will see you again and you will rejoice, and no one will take away your joy" (John 16:21–22).

When we let people save face, we are doing what is right and just, not being merely magnanimous and gracious.

5. We will protect them from their greatest fear.

When Joseph revealed his identity and expressed forgiveness, what do you suppose the eleven brothers were thinking? They were no doubt thrilled that their brother really and truly accepted them. The relief must have been sweet beyond words. But no sooner had they absorbed the good news than they experienced the greatest fear of all: they would have to return to Canaan and tell their father the truth of what they did.

> "Sin that is under the blood of our sovereign Redeemer does not need to be confessed to anyone but God."

You can be sure that they would rather have died than face their aged father with the truth behind that bloodstained coat of many colors that had been laid before him. For years, their worst nightmare had been that their father would find out about their deception. Now they were faced with the prospect of returning to Canaan to persuade their father to move to Egypt where his beloved Joseph was—would you believe—the prime minister. Jacob would certainly wonder how such a miracle was possible.

Joseph, knowing their guilt and dread, had already anticipated this problem and was a step ahead of his brothers. He knew that his forgiveness of what they had done was utterly worthless to them if they had to tell the whole truth to their father.

This to me is one of the most moving scenes in this story. Joseph instructed his brothers to tell their father the truth—that he, Joseph, was alive and well and had become the prime minister of Egypt. Indeed, he told them exactly what to say and what *not* to say to Jacob. His direction was worded carefully, and it told their father all of the truth that he needed to know. (See Genesis 45:9–13.)

Sin that is under the blood of our sovereign Redeemer does not need to be confessed to anyone but God. If you need to share your situation with one other person for therapeutic purposes, fine. But you should not involve an innocent person by unloading information on them that they can easily live without. Instead, confess your sin to God.

> Against you, you only, have I sinned and done what is evil in your sight, so that you are proved right when you speak and justified when you judge.
>
> —Psalm 51:4

You may think the brothers should have confessed their sin to their father. Really? Wouldn't that have given Jacob an even greater problem—having to struggle with the regret of lost years with Joseph and with bitterness against his other sons?

Joseph was wise, loving, and fair. And it made his brothers respect him all the more.

When I consider the fact that our Lord Jesus Christ knows all about my sin but promises to keep what He has forgiven a carefully guarded secret, it increases my gratitude to Him. Joseph, through his act of total forgiveness, endeared himself to his brothers.

"To hold another person in perpetual fear by threatening, "I'll tell on you," will quickly bring down the wrath of God."

Many of us have one single greatest fear. I know I do. I know what I would fear the most—were it to be told. But God has no desire to hold our fears over our heads. I am indebted to my wonderful Savior who forgives all of my sins and will ensure that my greatest fears will never be realized.

God does not blackmail us. And when a person is guilty of blackmailing someone else, it gets God's attention. He won't stand for it. To hold another person in perpetual fear by threatening, "I'll tell on you," will quickly bring down the wrath of God. When I ponder the sins for which I have been forgiven, it is enough to shut my mouth for the rest of my life.

6. It is a lifelong commitment.

Making a lifelong commitment to total forgiveness means that you keep on doing it—for as long as you live. It isn't enough to forgive today and then return to the offense tomorrow. I heard of a person whose wife said, "I thought you forgave me." He replied, "That was yesterday." Total forgiveness is a lifelong commitment, and you may need to practice it every single day of your life until you die. No one said it would be easy.

> "What Joseph had done seventeen years before still held good; he was prepared to care for his brothers indefinitely."

Seventeen years after reuniting with his long-lost son, Jacob died. Joseph's brothers suddenly panicked. They were terrified that Joseph's forgiveness would last only as long as their aged patriarch was still alive, that Joseph would at long last take revenge on them. We can understand their fears. Joseph's forgiveness was no ordinary thing; they had been incredibly blessed by his graciousness. But they feared it had come to an end: "When Joseph's brothers saw that their father was dead, they said, 'What if Joseph holds a grudge against us and pays us back for all the wrongs we did to him?'" (Gen. 50:15).

Because of their fear, they concocted a story:

> So they sent word to Joseph, saying, "Your father left these instructions before he died: 'This is what you are to say to Joseph: I ask you to forgive your brothers the sins and the

> wrongs they committed in treating you so badly.' Now please forgive the sins of the servants of the God of your father."
>
> —GENESIS 50:16–17

If Jacob had really said this, he would not have just told Joseph's brothers; he would have told Joseph himself before he died. He would not have gone to his grave with a fear that Joseph would not forgive them. It was the brothers who were afraid.

When Joseph heard this message, he wept. He could not believe that his brothers doubted him. He could see that they lived in fear that one day he, the prime minister, would use his power to take vengeance on his brothers.

> But Joseph said to them, "Don't be afraid. Am I in the place of God? You intended to harm me, but God intended it for good to accomplish what is now being done, the saving of many lives. So then, don't be afraid. I will provide for you and your children." And he reassured them and spoke kindly to them.
>
> —GENESIS 50:19–21

What Joseph had done seventeen years before still held good; he was prepared to care for his brothers indefinitely. "I forgave you then, and I forgive you now," he was saying to them. Joseph's change of heart was no passing thing. It was real. I have seen some people cave in and return to the offense after they extended their forgiveness to someone. But it is not total forgiveness unless it lasts—no matter how great the temptation is to turn back. I wonder if this is the "folly" that is referred to in Psalm 85:8: "I will listen to what God the LORD will say; he promises peace to his people, his saints—but let them not return to folly."

I know that in my own case the temptation to return to bitterness was very real. I would concoct conversations in my head, imagining what I might say or recalling what had taken place, and I would get churned up. The thought that "No one will ever know," or "They are getting away with this," would agitate me. But if I took a step back and observed the situation from a distance, I could see the folly of such thinking. I had to keep on forgiving. Total forgiveness must go on and on and on. Some days will be harder than others.

I must never tell what I know, cause my offenders to feel fear, make them feel guilty, hope they will lose face, or reveal their most devastating secrets. And I must keep this up as long as I live.

If you are prepared to make a covenant to forgive—and to forgive totally—you must realize you will have to renew that covenant tomorrow. And it may be even harder to do tomorrow than it is today. It could even be harder next week—or next year. But this is a lifetime commitment.

7. We will pray for them to be blessed.

Total forgiveness involves an additional element: praying for God's blessings to rain on the lives of your offenders. "But I tell you: Love your enemies and pray for those who persecute you" (Matt. 5:44). When you do this as Jesus intends it, you are being set free indeed.

To truly pray for the one who hurt you means to pray that they will be blessed, that God will show favor to them rather than punish them, that they will prosper in every way. In other words, you pray that they will be dealt with as you want God to deal with you. You apply the Golden Rule as you pray. (See Matthew 7:12.) You don't pray, "God, deal with them." You don't pray, "Lord, get them for what they did to me." And neither is it enough to say, "Father, I commend them to You." That's a cop-out. You must pray that they receive total forgiveness, just as you want it for yourself.

Praying like this, to quote John Calvin, "is exceedingly difficult." Chrysostom (c. 344–407) called it the very highest summit of self-control. And yet Job's suffering did not end until he prayed for those "friends" who had become his thorn in the flesh (Job 42:10). When we do this, we are becoming more like our heavenly Father. (See Matthew 5:44ff.) That is true godliness, the very essence of Christlikeness.

> "Total forgiveness involves an additional element: praying for God's blessings to rain on the lives of your offenders."

To me the greatest inspiration to live in this manner is found in the life—and death—of Stephen. He is one of my heroes. When I read Acts 6:8–15 and consider the Holy Spirit's touch on his life, his enemies' inability to contradict his wisdom, the miracles he did, and his radiant countenance, I say to myself, "I'd give anything in the world for that kind of anointing." His secret, however, emerged at the end of his life. While his enemies threw stones at him, he prayed—seconds before his last breath—"Lord, do not hold this sin against them" (Acts 7:60). And therein lies the secret to his unusual anointing.

If you are still asking, "How can I know that I have totally forgiven my enemy (my betrayer, my unfaithful spouse, my unkind parent, the one who ruined my life, or the one who has hurt our children)?" I answer, "Walking out these seven principles is as near as you can come to exhibiting *total forgiveness.*"

I must add one caution: never go to a person you have had to forgive and say, "I forgive you." This will be counterproductive every time unless it is to a person that you know is yearning for you to forgive them. Otherwise, you will create a stir with which you will not be able to cope. They will say to you, "For what?" It is my experience that nine out of ten people I have had to forgive sincerely do not feel they have done anything wrong. It is up to me to forgive them from my heart—and then keep quiet about it.

This is to my mind the best and clearest book that I have read on forgiveness. It has radically changed my life. I gave on loan to a friend who put it into application and in a very short time his family is being reconciled. Thank R.T.

—Fraser MacLeod
Dieulefit, France

3

THE LORD'S PRAYER AND FORGIVENESS

This, then, is how you should pray:

"Our Father in heaven,
hallowed be your name,
your kingdom come,
your will be done
on earth as it is in heaven.
Give us today our daily bread.
Forgive us our debts,
as we also have forgiven our debtors.
And lead us not into temptation
but deliver us from the evil one."

For if you forgive men when they sin against you, your heavenly Father will also forgive you. But if you do not forgive men their sins, your Father will not forgive your sins.

—*Matthew 6:9–15*

It may seem surprising to some that people who are not Christians can learn to forgive. I believe that there are degrees of forgiveness. A person who is not a Christian could demonstrate what may be called "limited forgiveness" and feel all the better for it. If a person is sufficiently motivated, he or she may achieve a great deal of inner satisfaction by overcoming bitterness. Mahatma Gandhi appealed to a sense of valor and heroism when he said, "The weak can never forgive. Forgiveness is the attribute of the strong." On the other hand, President John F. Kennedy said, "Forgive your enemies, but never forget their names." That is hardly total forgiveness!

The Bible urges us to forgive—totally. It is very surprising, therefore, to learn that there is no teaching of this kind of forgiveness in Judaism. After the Holocaust, there was a consensus that the Jewish people would never forget—ever. The idea of a Jew becoming a believer in Jesus as the Messiah and then praying with a Palestinian believer is unthinkable for the majority of Jews today. But that is happening—even in Israel. One wishes that this sort of thing would happen in Gentile Christian churches, where bitterness is often justified!

"Forgive Us Our Debts"

I suppose that the fifth petition of the Lord's Prayer, "Forgive us our debts as we also have forgiven our debtors"—or, as put another way, "Forgive us our trespasses as we forgive those who trespass against us"—has made liars out of more people than any other line in human history. But don't blame Jesus for that. We should mean what we say if we choose to pray the Lord's Prayer. And

Jesus did not say we had a choice; He said, "This, then, is how you should pray."

Jesus regarded this as the most important petition in His prayer. "Forgive us our debts" is obviously a plea for forgiveness from God. But then comes the following line (or possibly the big lie): "as we also have forgiven our debtors." This petition is both a plea for forgiveness and a claim that we have already forgiven those who hurt us. In Luke's version of the account, Jesus says, "Forgive us our sins, for we also forgive everyone who sins against us" (Luke 11:4). There the verb *forgive* is in the present tense; when we pray in that manner, we are claiming that we are forgiving everyone.

> "We should mean what we say if we choose to pray the Lord's Prayer."

I have prayed that this teaching will make a difference in the lives of those who read it. That means I have prayed for you. I have a suspicion that there are many reading this book who do not necessarily need this teaching—and there are some who need it desperately. I don't want you to have pseudoguilt about this issue. I don't want to cause anyone to feel condemned or threatened. But if you can take this word and apply it, I believe this teaching can make a difference in your life.

When you pray this petition, "Forgive us our trespasses as we forgive those who trespass against us," you are asking God to forgive all of your sins. The word translated "debt," or "trespasses," comes from a Greek word that simply means "what is owed." It is used interchangeably with the word *sins*. Just after the prayer is finished, Jesus goes on to say, "If you forgive men when they *sin* against you..." Jesus intended the meaning of *sin* when He said the word *debt*. It means "what is owed to God," and because you owe Him pure obedience, falling short of that means you are indebted to Him. In the Lord's Prayer, we ask Him to wipe that debt from our records.

When you pray, "*Forgive* us our debts," or "*Forgive* us our trespasses," you are asking God to let you off the hook. To "forgive" comes from a Greek word that means "to let be" or "to send away." For example, "to let be" would mean that God would not do anything to punish you; He would just let you stay as you are and wipe away what you owe. "To send away" means that your sins would be cast away from you and you would not be liable for them; instead of your having to pay, God just lets the debt go.

> "Walking in the light means following without compromise *anything God shows you to do.*"

This line, however, is not a prayer for salvation. It is not what we call the "sinner's prayer," which is summed up in the words "God, be merciful to me, a sinner" and is essentially the way a person comes to Christ. (See Luke 18:13.) If we pleaded for salvation on the basis that we had already forgiven others, then our salvation would be conditional; we would deserve it if we had forgiven others and not deserve it if we hadn't. That is, it would be as if, once we had forgiven everyone, God would say, "OK, now I will save you." But then we could only maintain our salvation as long as we continued forgiving everyone. If we ever stopped, then we would lose our salvation. So if the Lord's Prayer were a prayer for the non-Christian to pray, it would be a prayer for a conditional salvation—based on good works.

On the contrary, these words constitute a prayer that only a believer—one who can truly call God "Father"—can pray. The truth is, Jesus Himself acknowledges what the Bible generally affirms:

> Who can say, "I have kept my heart pure; I am clean and without sin"?
>
> —Proverbs 20:9

> There is not a righteous man on earth who does what is right and never sins.
>
> —Ecclesiastes 7:20

> There is no one who does not sin.
>
> —1 Kings 8:46

> If we claim to be without sin, we deceive ourselves and the truth is not in us.
>
> —1 John 1:8

What Is the Purpose of the Lord's Prayer?

What, then, is the purpose of this prayer? It is not to appeal to our own strength, but to keep us in fellowship with the Father: "But if we walk in the light, as he is in the light, we have fellowship with one another, and the blood of Jesus, his Son, purifies us from all sin" (1 John 1:7).

In order to have fellowship with the Father, because God is light and in Him there is no darkness at all (1 John 1:5), all of our sin must be cleansed. Walking in the light means following without compromise *anything God shows you to do*. But if He shows you something and you sweep it under the carpet, years later you will wonder why you haven't grown spiritually. The reason will be because you postponed obedience; there was no real fellowship with the Father.

The Lord's Prayer is designed to keep us from having a self-righteous attitude. We all have this problem, and most of us fight it every day. We naturally want to justify ourselves; we instinctively want to point the finger. This prayer helps to keep us on our toes spiritually and gives us objectivity about ourselves. This prayer shows us that we need daily forgiveness as much as we need daily bread.

There are two things Jesus takes for granted in the Lord's Prayer: that people have hurt us, and that we ourselves will need to be forgiven. We have all come short of *God's* glory, and often other people come short of treating *us* with the dignity, love, and respect that we would like. We have hurt God, and we want to be let off the hook; people have hurt us, and we must let them off the hook.

"This prayer shows us that we need daily forgiveness as much as we need daily bread."

In what ways have you been hurt by other people? Perhaps you have been discredited or dishonored; maybe you have been disappointed that people could be so ungrateful. You may have been lied about or taken advantage of; people may not have been very appreciative; they may have been disloyal. Think of someone in your life who has discredited you. Think of someone in your life who has disappointed you because they were not grateful. Jesus is telling us that's the way people are.

You may not realize it, but you do the same thing to other people. Wouldn't you like them to let *you* off the hook? You pray that God won't throw the book at you, and yet you pray that God will throw the book at them.

Once, at a critical time in my life, I wanted to get closer to God—but I also knew that I had to forgive someone who had wronged me. It was as though God stopped me in midsentence and said, "RT, do you know what you are asking? This means you are wanting Me to forgive them and to bless them." It is one thing to say "Forgive them" to God and yet hope that He doesn't, but it is another thing to say it and mean it. In that moment, I had to decide. Did I want God to take me seriously, to truly forgive them and let them off the hook?

Do you want God to let *you* off the hook? As I previously mentioned, we've all got skeletons in our closets. What if God decided, because you refused to forgive another person, that He would pull a skeleton out of your closet and let everyone else know what He knows about you? That is a pretty good motivation, if you ask me, to say, "God, forgive them. Yes, thank You very much. Please forgive them."

A Clear Path

Not only do we need daily forgiveness as much as we need daily bread, but we also need to pray daily that we have the grace to forgive others as a lifelong commitment. It is not easy. No one ever said it would be. It has been the hardest thing I have ever had to do, but following this phrase in the Lord's Prayer is the clearest path to fellowship with God. There is no forgiveness for the one who does not forgive, but it is not a prayer for justification. Neither is it a prayer for keeping yourself saved. It is a prayer for continued fellowship. It means no pointing of the finger, no keeping a record of wrongs.

As soon as Jesus finished teaching His disciples the Lord's Prayer, He added:

> For if you forgive men when they sin against you, your heavenly Father will also forgive you.
>
> —Matthew 6:14

It is as though Jesus added a PS to the Lord's Prayer: "For *if* you forgive men when they sin against you, your heavenly Father will also forgive you." It almost seems that that is why He gave us the prayer in the first place!

Why does Jesus, when He is demonstrating which of the petitions was the most important, add this further statement? The most natural tendency in the world is to want to get even when someone has offended you. It is as natural as eating or sleeping, and it is instinctual. Jesus is telling us to do something that is not natural but supernatural: totally forgiving people—sometimes those closest to us—for the wrongs they do to us. I still struggle in this area myself. But when I truly and totally forgive, I have crossed over into the supernatural—and have achieved an accomplishment equal to any miracle.

> "Not only do we need daily forgiveness as much as we need daily bread, but we also need to pray daily that we have the grace to forgive others as a lifelong commitment."

The kingdom of heaven is the domain of the Holy Spirit. When the Holy Spirit is at home in us, it means He is not grieved. He can be Himself; He isn't adjusting to us, but we are adjusting to Him. When Jesus said, "If you forgive men when they sin against you, your heavenly Father will also forgive you," He was not talking about how to achieve salvation. He was referring to receiving the anointing of God and participating in an intimate relationship with the Father. Unless we are walking in a state of forgiveness toward others, we cannot be in an intimate relationship with God.

Being Honest With Ourselves About Bitterness

Here's an even harder truth. John says, "If we claim to have fellowship with him yet walk in the darkness, we lie and do not live by the truth" (1 John 1:6). One way we walk in darkness is by holding bitterness in our hearts toward others—bitterness that creates confusion in our minds and oppression in our hearts. You may say, "Oh, but I am having fellowship with God." No, you're not. You're just claiming you are having fellowship with God if there is bitterness in your heart. And if we claim to have fellowship with God but walk in darkness, we lie.

Walking in darkness is the consequence of unforgiveness. When I don't forgive, I might spend hours a day in prayer, but I am not having genuine fellowship with God. If I can't forgive the person who hurt someone dear to me, I am walking in darkness. If I can't forgive the person who lied about me to others, I have lost my intimate relationship with the Father. I can even continue to preach, and people may even say, "Oh, what a wonderful sermon! You must be so close to God!" I can sing praises to the Lord with my hands in the air, and you may say, "Oh, look at how RT is worshiping the Lord!" I could put on such an act that you would think that I am the holiest person in the church. But if I have bitterness inside or am holding a grudge against someone else, I am a liar. I cannot walk in the light when I am really in darkness.

Jesus tenderly shows us in the Lord's Prayer that we will be hurt—and by people we never dreamed would hurt us. We might think, "Well, yes, I can imagine so-and-so hurting me, but I never thought it would be you!" Psalm 41:9 candidly predicts what Jesus warns us of: "Even my close friend, whom I trusted, he who shared my bread, has lifted up his heel against me." We will be hurt by the people we love. What's more, Jesus calls the acts that they do against us "sin."

When people don't mean to hurt

Now, there is more than one kind of wound that causes hurt and pain. In some cases people disappoint you by doing things they think are necessary. They don't intend to hurt you, but they do. As a parent or church leader, you sometimes do this—you must make a decision and then say, "I'm sorry, but this is the way it has to be."

> "The greater the sin you must forgive, the greater the measure of the Spirit that will come to you."

People in my life have made these kinds of decisions. Even though wounding me was not their motive, they knew their decisions would hurt me, and they did. In these cases, the offense is not an outright sin you must forgive, but you are hurt nonetheless.

Hurt caused by insensitivity

On the other hand, there are people in our world whose actions are called "sin." And again, there is more than one kind of such sin. There are sins that are not willfully committed but nonetheless are done without any sensitivity toward the feelings of others. A person can be so full of himself—due to his own anger or ambition—that he or she hurts other people without realizing it. Never forget that you might have hurt others unwittingly; we all sin every day, and we therefore should pray daily for those we have hurt without even knowing it.

We must learn to foster a spirit of sensitivity to those around us. The more sensitive I am to the Holy Spirit, the more aware

I will be of people around me who are in pain. Remember the words written about Jesus: "A bruised reed he will not break" (Matt. 12:20). I want to treat every single person I meet in that manner, but I fear I do not always do that. So there is one kind of sin where the offenders are not malicious, they are not hateful, and their motive is not to hurt, but they still sin through their insensitivity to others.

Hurt caused by sins knowingly committed

But there are also sins that are willfully committed. Some people do wicked things with their eyes wide open, and these people surely have to know they have done something wrong. You may say, "Do I have to forgive even that?" The answer is yes.

There is a wonderful consolation, however: the greater the sin you must forgive, the greater the measure of the Spirit that will come to you. So if you have an extremely difficult situation on your hands and you say, "I can't forgive this!" you may not realize at first that there, handed to you on a silver platter, is an opportunity to receive a measure of anointing that someone else might not ever get! Consider it a challenge and an opportunity; take it with both hands. Welcome the opportunity to forgive the deepest hurt, the greatest injustice, and remember that a greater anointing is waiting for you.

What sin is it that we must forgive? Any sin that has been committed against us. We must begin by not judging. It is not for us to judge another's motives. Reserving judgment for God alone shows that we are already beginning to forgive. We must leave to God how guilty our offenders are before Him. We may not know whether what they did was deliberate—we can only know for certain that we were hurt. It may be that our offenders are the way they are because of bad parenting when they were children. I am sure that all of our children sooner or later will realize where we as parents have failed and will need to forgive us. I have had to forgive my dad for his imperfections. Perhaps you have had to forgive that unfair schoolteacher, that incompetent boss. Moreover, you must also forgive a fellow Christian who has been insensitive.

Jesus is talking about a chosen privilege. "If you forgive men"—that is, if you *choose* to do it. You can choose not to. "A man's wisdom gives him patience; it is to his glory to overlook an offense" (Prov. 19:11). Can you think of many other things that can bring glory? Having your funeral conducted at Westminster Abbey? Being knighted? Winning a gold medal in the Olympics? Winning the Nobel Peace Prize? That may be glory, but Proverbs 19:11 says, "It is to a man's glory to overlook an offense." That is far more spectacular in God's eyes than winning any Olympic competition. It is glory *to overlook an offense*. It requires a crossing-over into the supernatural.

Total Forgiveness Is a Chosen Privilege

Total forgiveness is a chosen privilege. It is a privilege to be godly—to be like God and to pass this forgiveness on to someone else. Why should you want to forgive? Because you prize intimacy and fellowship with the Father more than you desire to see your enemy being punished. You want God's anointing too much to pursue getting even.

But Jesus also puts it the other way around, just in case we didn't get the point already: "But if you do not forgive men their sins, your Father will not forgive your sins" (Matt. 6:15).

> "Even though we do not achieve salvation through our works, we are required to do good works, and one of those is forgiving those who have hurt us."

This, then, is the continuation of our Lord's postscript after the Lord's Prayer. We are hemmed in; there is no way we can avoid it. Forgiving people is serious business; it's not optional. And yet in order to motivate us to forgive, Jesus must say, "If you do not forgive, your Father will not forgive you."

What Happens When We Don't Forgive?

What, then, is the result if we do not forgive?

If it means that we lose our salvation, it follows that we must be saved by works. Make no mistake about it: when you forgive another person, that is a work—and it is a good work. But I would remind you that the apostle Paul said, "For it is by grace you have been saved, through faith—and this not from yourselves, it is the gift of God—not by works, so that no one can boast" (Eph. 2:8–9). But Paul adds, "For we are God's workmanship, created in Christ Jesus to do good works, which God prepared in advance for us to do" (v. 10). Even though we do not achieve salvation through our works, we are required to do good works, and one of those is forgiving those who have hurt us.

Although we know we are *saved* by grace alone, there remain consequences if we choose to walk in unforgiveness. Some aspects of our relationship with God are unchangeable, but others are affected by the things that we do.

1. Salvation is unconditional; fellowship with the Father is conditional.

When we are justified before God, we are declared righteous, and that comes by faith. Anyone who transfers the trust that he or she had in their good works—and trusts what Jesus did on the cross—is credited by God with perfect righteousness. But fellowship with the Father on the way to heaven is conditional. Unconfessed sin—including unforgiveness—in our lives can block our fellowship with the Father.

2. Justification before God is unconditional; the anointing of the Spirit is conditional.

The anointing—the power of the Spirit in our lives—may ebb and flow. The Dove may come down and then flutter away for a while, but our standing before God, because of the righteousness of Christ put to our credit (Rom. 4:4–5), is permanent.

3. Our status in the family of God is unconditional; our intimacy with Christ is conditional.

We are sons and daughters of the Most High once we have been adopted into God's family. (See Ephesians 1:5.) We are as secure in the family of God as Jesus Himself is in the Trinity.

Why? We have been made joint heirs with Christ (Rom. 8:17). We are saved, but our intimacy with Christ is conditional.

4. Our eternal destiny—whether we go to heaven or to hell—is fixed, but receiving an additional reward is conditional.

Once we are saved we are assured that we will go to heaven. But receiving an inheritance, a further reward, is conditional. Some may go to heaven without a reward: "If what he has built survives, he will receive his reward. If it is burned up, he will suffer loss; he himself will be saved, but only as one escaping through the flames" (1 Cor. 3:14–15).

Thank God all this is true, or there would be few, if any, ever saved! Yet having said that, totally forgiving another person is an achievable act. It can be done, and it is something you and I must keep doing. It's not enough to say, "Well, I did it yesterday. I have paid my dues. I showed I could do it." It is a lifelong commitment. But let no one say, "That's beyond me!" It can be done. It may be a continual struggle, but we do have the power to overcome—and the consequences are wonderful.

God Condemns an Unforgiving Spirit

God condemns an unforgiving spirit. "If you do not forgive men their sins, your Father will not forgive your sins," Jesus said. Why do you suppose God so hates an unforgiving spirit? There are three reasons.

1. It shows an indifference to the greatest thing God did.

This "greatest thing" was God sending His Son to die on the cross for our sins. To be forgiven is the most wonderful thing in the world. But in order to forgive us, God paid a severe price. I predict that when we get to heaven we will be able to see, little by little, what it meant for God to send His Son to die on a cross. We now only see the tip of the iceberg. We see waves of glory, and these overcome us, but we've seen little. God did for us what we did not deserve. He therefore wants us to pass this on to others who don't deserve it.

2. We interrupt God's purpose in the world: reconciliation.

God loves reconciliation. He has given the ministry of reconciliation to us, and He wants it to continue. When we are forgiven, He wants us to pass it on. When we interrupt that, He doesn't like it at all. He sent His Son to die on a cross, effectually calling us by His grace and giving us total forgiveness. But we interrupt that flow by not passing it on.

3. God hates ingratitude.

God knows the sins for which He has forgiven us, and He loves a grateful response. Matthew 18 relates the story of a servant who owed a great debt. He fell on his knees before his creditor, his master, and said, "Be patient and I will pay you back everything." The master took pity on him, canceling the debt and letting him go. The master knew the things for which he had forgiven his servant. But then that same servant went out and found one of his own servants who owed him a much smaller amount; he grabbed the man and began to choke him, saying, "Pay back what you owe!" The fellow servant did exactly what *he himself* had done; he fell on his knees and said, "Please forgive me. I will pay you back." But the one who had been forgiven a much greater debt refused to extend forgiveness, and he threw his servant into prison. To think there could be such ingratitude! Word eventually reached the original master, and the unforgiving servant was also thrown into debtor's prison.

> "Totally forgiving another person is an achievable act. It can be done, and it is something you and I must keep doing."

Jesus then added, "This is how my heavenly Father will treat each of you unless you forgive your brother from your heart" (Matt. 18:35). God knows what we have done. He knows the sins for which He has forgiven us, the things that no one else will ever hear about. If we turn around and say, "I can't forgive that person for what he has done," God doesn't like it at all. He hates ingratitude.

How Unforgiveness Manifests Itself

Having an unforgiving spirit usually begins with resentment. Resentment is seen when a person holds a grudge and becomes inwardly bitter. They become preoccupied with hate and self-pity. They can't come to terms with the possibility that the person who committed such an awful act against them will not get caught.

They want them exposed; they want them to be held up for the whole world to see what they have done.

Resentment leads to going over and over again in your mind what the offender did, recounting and reliving exactly what happened. You should not dwell on the incident or even think about it. It will not bring you any relief or release; instead, it will cause you to become even more churned up.

All of this leads to wanting to get even, to take revenge. You become determined to make your offender pay, not unlike the servant who had been forgiven a great debt but who still said, "Pay me back; pay me back!" He had been forgiven, but he couldn't pass that forgiveness on to another.

How do you make your enemies pay for their crimes against you? One way is to threaten to tell what you know about them and keep them paralyzed with fear. Perhaps you know a dirty secret about someone who offended you, and if you spilled the beans it could ruin their life. It would be gratifying to dangle such knowledge over their head every so often and say, "I still might tell." But would Jesus do that? Do you have any idea how much it upsets God when you or I behave like that?

There will be a payday for those who won't forgive others. "But if you do not forgive men their sins, your Father will not forgive your sins" (Matt. 6:15). God is displeased when you or I hold another person hostage in fear, knowing of what He has forgiven us.

"Making a choice to continue in unforgiveness shows that we aren't sufficiently grateful for God's forgiveness of our own sins."

We may also seek our revenge by hurting that person's reputation by keeping others from thinking well of them. We may even take the punishment further and administer justice personally, trying to mete out the most severe penalty available to us. Never mind that God says, "Vengeance is Mine!" Never mind that God says, "This is something that only I do." If *we* do it—let me make you a promise—it will only be one-tenth of what *God* would have done. If you and I can't wait on God's timing and His manner, and we say, "I'm going to make sure justice is carried out," God says, "You're on your own."

Forgiveness is a choice we must make, and it is not a choice that comes easily. If it were easy, why do you think Jesus would mention it again after He finished the Lord's Prayer? He knows forgiveness is difficult. It wasn't easy for God to do what He did either, but He did it anyway. He sacrificed His Son, and He asks us to make a little sacrifice in return. We must make the choice to let our enemies off the hook and even *pray* that God will let them off the hook. When you do that and really mean it, *you are there*. He looks down from heaven and says, "Good." But then you have to do it again tomorrow. You must make the choice and live it out. Love is an act of the will.

Making a choice to continue in unforgiveness shows that we aren't sufficiently grateful for God's forgiveness of our own sins. Perhaps we haven't taken seriously enough our own sin or our own redemption. Probably what we all want to say is, "Well, what I did wasn't nearly as bad as what they have done!" And that's where we are wrong! God hates self-righteousness as much as He hates the injustice that you think is so horrible, and He certainly doesn't like it when we judge. So if you must forget the sins of which God has forgiven you, at least remember that one of the most heinous sins of all is self-righteousness.

I will never forget the time that this hit me. Some years ago I saw for the first time John Newton's hymn:

> In evil long I took delight,
> Unawed by shame or fear,
> Till a new object struck my sight,
> And stopped my wild career.[1]

When I read these words I suddenly realized that I had had a wild career of being self-righteous, taking myself too seriously; I felt so ashamed.

Realize this: as much as God hates self-righteousness, He will forgive us of that sin, too! You may say, "I haven't had a sexual thought about that person" or "I haven't fallen into immorality like that person." Sexual sins *are* serious business, no doubt. But to God, the sin of self-righteousness is much worse.

One primary cause of an unforgiving spirit is self-righteousness. When we understand the magnitude of the sins of which we were forgiven, we cannot help but be grateful for what God has done, and it becomes easy to forgive other people.

Not Valuing Our Fellowship With the Father

There is, however, another cause for unforgiveness: that we don't put a high enough value on our fellowship with the Father. There should be nothing more important to us than our relationship with God. The apostle John said, "And our fellowship is with the Father and with his Son, Jesus Christ" (1 John 1:3). Do you put a high value on your times of fellowship with the Father? Moreover, does receiving a reward in heaven mean little or nothing to you? If you choose to withhold forgiveness from others, you are not putting a high enough value on things today that one day will mean everything to you.

The Consequences of an Unforgiving Spirit

What, then, are the consequences of harboring unforgiveness in our hearts? What exactly did Jesus mean when He said, "But if you do not forgive men their sins, your Father will not forgive your sins" (Matt. 6:15)?

1. The Holy Spirit is grieved.

"And do not grieve the Holy Spirit of God, with whom you were sealed for the day of redemption" (Eph. 4:30). Your relationship with the Holy Spirit should be one of the most important priorities in your life. When the Holy Spirit is grieved, it causes a distortion in our thinking. The ungrieved Spirit is what enables us to cope. I would not be able to do my job if the Holy Spirit were permanently grieved with me. I would not be able to function or think clearly. If I have spoken a sharp word to my wife, Louise, or to my kids or someone around me, or if I have harbored feelings of resentment, trying to prepare a sermon is impossible. Why? My attitude grieves the Spirit.

> "A refusal to forgive means that God stands back and lets you cope with your problems in your own strength."

It is no different for you. You want to be at your best, whether working with computers; being a teacher, lawyer, doctor, or nurse; or simply typing a letter. You do not want the Holy Spirit to be upset with you. Let's not forget that immediately after Paul admonished us not to grieve the Spirit, he added:

> Get rid of all bitterness, rage and anger, brawling and slander, along with every form of malice. Be kind and compassionate to one another, forgiving each other, just as in Christ God forgave you.
>
> —EPHESIANS 4:31–32

2. You are left to yourself.

A refusal to forgive means that God stands back and lets you cope with your problems in your own strength. Not many people want to live that kind of life—coping on their own without God's help. Personally, I couldn't bear it. The Bible says the backslider is "filled with his own ways" (Prov. 14:14, KJV), so when one is left to oneself and to the flesh, those unthinkable capabilities toward sin in that person are given free reign. Not only that, but Satan is also able to get in. He will take advantage of us if he can. (See

2 Corinthians 2:11.) He will exploit that unforgiving spirit, play on your self-pity, and, worst of all, cause you to fancy that God is with you in this!

It's like when the devil said to Eve, "You will not surely die" (Gen. 3:4), and she said, in effect, "Oh, well, thank you for that!" She believed him. The devil will come around and say, "Now look, normally it would be true that you should forgive, but what you have had to forgive is much worse than anybody else's offenses, so God exempts you." And you say, "Oh, thank you for that!" and are silly enough to believe it.

> "The reason God treats you like an enemy is because, by not forgiving others, you are really saying, "God, move over; I want to do Your job!""

First, then, the Holy Spirit is grieved and you are not able to think clearly. Second, the devil gains access because God leaves you to yourself. But you still begin to fancy that God is with you—that you are perfectly justified in your anger. Once that has happened, do not be surprised if at the end of the day you fall into other sins. You may even begin to do things that you never thought you would do. Once the devil gains entrance, you begin to compromise all sorts of things relating to money, sex, and integrity. I once knew a man who fell into sexual immorality, but the true beginning of the root of sin in his life was his bitterness. Bitterness may seem a thousand miles from sexual immorality, but this man didn't forgive the one who had wronged him, and eventually he fell into sexual immorality. Why? He was left to himself.

3. You force God to become your enemy.

> What causes fights and quarrels among you? Don't they come from your desires that battle within you? You want something but don't get it. You kill and covet, but you cannot have what you want. You quarrel and fight. You do not have, because you do not ask God. When you ask, you do not receive, because you ask with wrong motives, that you may spend what you get on your pleasures.
>
> You adulterous people, don't you know that friendship with the world is hatred toward God? Anyone who chooses to be a friend of the world becomes an enemy of God.
>
> —James 4:1–4

The reason God treats you like an enemy is because, by not forgiving others, you are really saying, "God, move over; I want to do Your job!" You crown yourself judge, jury, and executioner, and you presume to take God's place. He alone is the righteous Judge. Being righteous, He will do right. He will clear your name. He will deal fairly with those who hurt you. He feels what you feel. But if you decide to do His work for Him, He becomes your enemy. Whenever we judge another, we never get away with it. Do not judge, and you won't be judged. Judge, and you will be judged. It's as simple as that.

4. You lose the potential of your anointing.

When you will not forgive, the anointing God may have given to you is lifted, and you will become like an empty shell. You may be able to continue for a while, because the gifts of God are irrevocable. (See Romans 11:29.) Even King Saul prophesied for a while after the Spirit left him, but eventually he lost everything.

Next to my salvation, I regard the anointing as the most precious thing I have on this earth. I do not want to lose the anointing of God. We may flourish for a while; the momentum of other gifts in us may make us think we still have the anointing we enjoyed yesterday. But mark this down: bearing a grudge and trying to punish and get even will cut off your anointing. The loss will become apparent sooner or later—unless you choose to forgive, and forgive totally.

5. No authentic fellowship with the Father

What often happens when we don't forgive is that we begin to live in a dream world. We are in a deep sleep and don't know it until we wake up and say, "Oh, I fell asleep!" When we are in a deep sleep, we may do things that we would never do while wide-awake. I would like this chapter to be a wake-up call. Are you like the Prodigal Son who eventually "came to his senses" (Luke 15:17)? It is a serious matter: "If we claim to have fellowship with him yet walk in the darkness, we lie and do not live by the truth" (1 John 1:6).

> **"When you will not forgive, the anointing God may have given to you is lifted, and you will become like an empty shell."**

Jesus said, "If you do not forgive men their sins, your Father will not forgive your sins." Harsh as this sounds, there is a tender phrase that can be found in this verse: "your Father." God is still your Father, no matter how many times you sin against Him.

When it comes to forgiveness of sins, then, there are two levels. One is what you would call forensic; it refers to what is legal and is the essence of being justified. God legally declares that we are righteous. It is the way God sees us in Christ—legally, as if we had never sinned. But there is also the spiritual level, wherein we are not only declared righteous, but we also enjoy a spiritual experience that comes from being forgiven. It is this experience that you lose when you are in a state of unforgiveness.

Why did Jesus give this word in His model prayer? He did it to motivate us. It's a warning we all must heed. And if a person who is not a Christian can be motivated to forgive, even if only in a limited way, how much more should we as Christians be motivated by the Holy Spirit to forgive—totally?

This book has totally changed my life. RT Kendall offers an amazing piece of work that, as you discover from the book, was born out of his own personal experience. The book is full of practical teaching about what our misconceptions of forgiveness are and what true Godly forgiveness is. This is not a book that tries to being a complex formula to forgiveness but rather it tries to explain from biblical concepts the importance of choosing to forgive those who have hurt us and our loved ones. I read it on the recommendation of a friend and have been thoroughly blessed.

—William Powell
Ft. Benning, GA

4

PLAYING GOD

Do not judge, or you too will be judged. For in the same way you judge others, you will be judged, and with the measure you use, it will be measured to you.
—Matthew 7:1–2

I could take you to the very spot—a table in the Duke Humphrey wing of the Bodleian Library in Oxford. I was in the process of discovering the works of the great William Perkins (1558–1602), an Elizabethan Puritan. I came in that day feeling very discouraged and inferior compared to the other students at Oxford University. Here I was from the hills of Kentucky, a place not exactly known for its centers of academic excellence. "You don't belong here," my mind suggested—and at that point, my eyes fell on these words of William Perkins: "Don't believe the devil, even when he tells the truth."

The devil was playing God that day. He loves to play God, and he wants us to join him in playing God as well.

When Jesus said, "Be perfect, therefore, as your heavenly Father is perfect" (Matt. 5:48), He was setting the stage for a higher level of perfection than many Christians have even thought to strive for. What we see in Jesus's words, "Do not judge, or you too will be judged," is an example of this level of perfection—not the sinless perfection of Christ, but a level of maturity that allows us to have a true intimacy with God and a greater anointing. Matthew 5:7 tells us, "Blessed are the merciful, for they will be shown mercy," because being merciful is showing graciousness. Paul said, "Let your gentleness be evident to all" (Phil. 4:5).

As we saw above, the word *gentleness* in this passage comes from a Greek word that literally means "to be gracious." When you could throw the book at somebody but instead you show mercy, you are making the choice to be gracious.

Judging is the opposite of graciousness. Being gracious is the consequence of a choice. Remember that any time you choose to judge, you are not being gracious. Judging someone else is actually uncalled-for criticism. That's what Jesus means by judging. When Jesus says, "Do not judge," He is not telling us to ignore what is wrong. He is saying not to administer any uncalled-for criticism; that is, criticism that is unfair or unjustified.

One acrostic that I have found helpful is built on the word NEED. When speaking to or about another person, ask yourself if what you are about to say will meet their need:

- ▹ **N**ecessary—Is it necessary to say this?
- ▹ **E**ncourage—Will this encourage them? Will it make them feel better?

- ▹ **E**dify—Will it edify? Will what you say build them up and make them stronger?
- ▹ **D**ignify—Will it dignify that person? Jesus treated other people with a sense of dignity.

Criticism that is either unfair or unjust, *even if it is true*, should not be uttered. The fact that what you would say is true does not necessarily make it right to say. Often Satan's accusations are true; he is an expert at being a judge. He is even called "the accuser of our brothers" (Rev. 12:10). You may be pointing your finger and speaking words of truth, but you may unwittingly be an instrument of the devil as you speak.

The word *judge* comes from the Greek word *krino*, which basically means "to make a distinction." Making a distinction between two things is often a good thing to do. Being discriminate can be prudent, and it can be wise. The apostle Paul said, "The spiritual man makes judgments about all things" (1 Cor. 2:15). We are told to make righteous judgments. But what Jesus is talking about here is judging *people* and unfairly criticizing them. It is our way of playing God.

You might be interested to know that I have probably worked harder on this particular chapter than on any other chapter in any book I have ever written! For years I have read Luke 6:37 every day; it says, "Do not judge, and you will not be judged." I made the decision many years ago to read it every day, and I still do. Every single day. Why have I chosen this particular verse to focus on? Because judging is probably my greatest weakness.

Judging other people is almost always counterproductive. When I judge someone else, I may be thinking, "What I want to do is change this person, straighten this person out." But it has the opposite effect almost every time! Sooner or later it will backfire. The other person will become offended, and the situation will not be resolved.

The degree to which we resist the temptation to judge will be the degree to which we ourselves are largely spared of being judged: "Do not judge, or you too will be judged." In Matthew, this statement is given as a warning, but in Luke it is given as a promise:

> Do not judge, and you will not be judged. Do not condemn, and you will not be condemned. Forgive, and you will be forgiven.
>
> —Luke 6:37

Being Critical of Others

Avoid dishing out criticism, then, and you will escape being criticized. Being judged is painful, whether or not the accusation is true. When we are criticized, we don't like it; it is painful, and it hurts. It is harder to say which is more painful: to be falsely accused or to be accused truthfully. Most of us don't like either situation.

> "The degree to which we resist the temptation to judge will be the degree to which we ourselves are largely spared of being judged."

In this verse recorded in Luke, Jesus teaches about judging by appealing again to our self-interest. But this should not surprise us. God often does this. He motivates us with the idea of what we can receive if we follow His instructions, and what we will receive if we don't. Here Jesus uses the Greek word *hina*, which means "purpose." It is often translated "in order that," as is implied in the King James Version: "Judge not, that ye be not judged." Jesus's true meaning is, "Judge not, in order that you will not be judged."

Jesus has given us a pragmatic reason not to judge. If you don't like being judged yourself, then stop judging other people. This obviously and immediately appeals to our self-interest.

We don't like being judged. As Somerset Maugham once said, "When people ask for criticism, they really want praise." Before this book ever reaches your hands, you may be sure that my close friends will have read it first. While I may appreciate their kind words, I *must* have their criticism. And critical words, however necessary, will hurt a bit!

God *could* throw the book at me at any time. But He *won't*—that is, unless He sees me pointing my finger at somebody else. Then God will say, "Sorry about this, RT, but I must step in and deal with you. You should know better." God Himself will see that I am judged if I judge others.

It is so easy to criticize. You don't need to read a book on how to develop a pointing finger. You don't need more education, a higher IQ, or a lot of experience to get good at it, and judging is certainly no sign you are more spiritual. It has often been said that a little bit of learning is a dangerous thing. Sometimes a little bit of spirituality is a dangerous thing as well, because one may be just spiritual enough to see what is wrong in others—and to point the finger. The true test of spirituality is being able *not* to point the finger!

You may say, "Well, I have got to say something or nobody else will!" So what if no one else does? The person you are judging likely doesn't want to hear it, so we are not really helping anyway. When they are judged, they usually will feel worse but not change their behavior. God's Word is a practical command. "Stop it!" He says.

> If you do away with the yoke of oppression, with the pointing finger and malicious talk, and if you spend yourselves on behalf of the hungry and satisfy the needs of the oppressed, then your light will rise in the darkness, and your night will become like the noonday.
>
> —Isaiah 58:9–10

Consider the atmosphere you live in when it is devoid of criticism. How pleasant it is when we all live in harmony! (See Psalm 133:1.) It is so sweet and so good. Now consider the pain that follows when someone is critical of you. If you don't like being criticized, don't criticize others! A lot of grief could be spared if people would learn to control their tongues.

> "The true test of spirituality is being able *not* to point the finger!"

Paul instructs us, "Let your conversation be always full of grace, seasoned with salt, so that you may know how to answer everyone" (Col. 4:6). Peter adds these words, "Do not repay evil with evil or insult with insult, but with blessing, because to this you were called so that you may inherit a blessing" (1 Pet. 3:9). Jesus Himself even said, "But I tell you that men will have to give account on the day of judgment for every careless word they have spoken" (Matt. 12:36). That is enough to scare me into watching what I say!

Uncalled-for criticism usually creates a defensive reaction in the other person that leads to a countercharge. If I judge you for something, you immediately say, "Yeah, but what about you? I saw you do this; I heard you say that!"

"Oh, no, I did not!"

"Oh, yes, you did!"

These conversations are almost always counterproductive. They also get God's attention.

Today's English Version translates Matthew 7:1, "Do not judge others, so that *God* will not judge you" (emphasis added). This is precisely what Jesus is teaching. It is God who will do the judging. Your immediate judge may well be the person who will retort, but even that may be God at work.

According to Jesus, this painful consequence is just and fair, for if someone judges us because we first judged them, we are getting what we deserve. They may not have deserved what we gave them, but we deserve what they have given us.

There are two levels of motivation for applying Jesus's words. The first, or lower, level is self-interest. Jesus appeals to this level first when He warns of God's judgment of those who judge. It is not necessarily a bad thing to be motivated by self-interest; Jesus even encouraged it.

But there is a higher level for which to strive—to avoid grieving the Holy Spirit. When we grieve the Spirit, we lose our presence of mind and our ability to think clearly. We may even lose our self-control:

> The tongue also is a fire, a world of evil among the parts of the body. It corrupts the whole person, sets the whole course of his life on fire, and is itself set on fire by hell.
>
> —James 3:6

All hell can break loose when we don't learn to control our tongues.

So the lower level of motivation is, spare yourself unnecessary trouble. The higher level is, don't grieve the Holy Spirit; maintain your continual communion with Him, flowing in the Spirit, walking in the Spirit.

"Jealousy is one of the hardest things on earth to see in yourself."

If you invite God to become involved in your life, He will. But the very moment you point the finger at another person, He will get involved in a way that you may not like. He may well begin to judge *you*—not them—for doing the judging. If I resent another person's getting away with something and escaping punishment, it's because I am jealous of their situation, that they would be shown mercy when they ought to receive justice.

Jealousy is one of the hardest things on earth to see in yourself. I can see it in you, but never in me! We wouldn't want to admit to a fault like that; we will deny it for as long as we can.

Jealousy sometimes springs from the fear that a person won't get justice. We all want mercy for ourselves but justice for others.

Nathan and David

Many times we want to judge another person because we are emotionally involved. And we can become emotionally involved just by hearing about something that irks us—something that appeals to our sense of self-righteousness. That is what happened when the prophet Nathan came to King David who, two years before, committed the sins of adultery and murder. Nathan didn't go to David the day after Bathsheba became pregnant, or even the week after Uriah the Hittite was killed. Because he had not gotten caught for two years, David probably thought, "I'm going to get away with this!" But then, unexpectedly, out of the blue, the prophet Nathan arrived:

"David, I need to say something to you!"

"Nathan, how good to see you! Come in; come in!" says David.

Nathan told David a parable, and then he came to the punch line:

> Now a traveler came to the rich man, but the rich man refrained from taking one of his own sheep or cattle to prepare a meal for the traveler who had come to him. Instead, he took the ewe lamb that belonged to the poor man and prepared it for the one who had come to him.
>
> —2 Samuel 12:4

David burned with anger toward the rich man, and he pronounced sentence on this gross injustice: "As surely as the Lord lives"—that's strong language, the taking of an oath—"the man who did this deserves to die! He must pay for that lamb four times over, because he did such a thing and had no pity" (2 Sam. 12:4–5).

And then Nathan said to David, "You are the man!" (v. 7).

David did not know that with his decree he had pronounced a sentence on himself. Nathan confirmed the sentence as well: "The sword will never depart from your house" (2 Sam. 12:10).

Judging Is God's Prerogative

Judging people is elbowing in on God's exclusive territory. As we have already seen, Deuteronomy 32:35 ("It is mine to avenge; I will repay") is quoted twice in the New Testament (Rom. 12:19; Heb. 10:30). That means, that's not *your* job! "That's My privilege," says God. Judging is God's prerogative, nobody else's. If we move in on His territory, God looks at us and says, "Really? You've got to be kidding." To move in on the territory of the eternal Judge will get His attention—but not the kind of attention we want!

The word *godliness* means "being like God," and there are certain aspects of God's character that He commands us to imitate. For example, we are commanded to live holy lives: "Be holy, because I am holy" (1 Pet. 1:16). We are commanded to show mercy to our neighbors: "Be merciful, just as your Father is merciful" (Luke 6:36). God wants us to walk in integrity. He wants us to walk in truth and sincerity. But there is an aspect of the character of God where there is *no trespassing allowed*, and the moment we begin to point our fingers at other people, we are on it—we are sinning. That aspect is being a judge.

If you and I are foolish enough to administer uncalled-for criticism, we should remember three things:

- God is listening.
- He knows the truth about us.
- He is ruthlessly fair.

As Malachi says:

> Then those who feared the Lord talked with each other, and the Lord listened and heard. A scroll of remembrance was written in his presence concerning those who feared the Lord and honored his name.
>
> —Malachi 3:16

> "Judging people is elbowing in on God's exclusive territory."

Never forget that God knows the truth about us! "Nothing in all creation is hidden from God's sight. Everything is uncovered and laid bare before the eyes of him to whom we must give account" (Heb. 4:13). How would you like it if, as you are pointing the finger at someone else, an angel from heaven showed up and said, "Stop! Here's what I know about *you*," and then he revealed your secret sins to the person you were judging? God could just do that. While you are busy pointing your finger, God may be looking down from heaven with the angels and saying, "I can't believe he would talk that way, because we know all about *him*!"

David had forgotten what he had done until Nathan came to him. We too may begin to think, "All is well; I am serving the Lord." We may forget the sins of which we have been forgiven. But God is still gracious. The fact that He is using any of us in His kingdom doesn't mean we are perfect.

Here are two practical verses that we all would do well to consider:

> Do not pay attention to every word people say, or you may hear your servant cursing you.
>
> —Ecclesiastes 7:21

> Do not revile the king even in your thoughts, or curse the rich in your bedroom, because a bird of the air may carry your words, and a bird on the wing may report what you say.
>
> —Ecclesiastes 10:20

God has a way of exposing us just when we begin to think, "There is no way that could happen to me." The Lord promises that equitable judgment will be administered. The word *equitable* means "fair" or "just." All of God's judgments are ruthlessly fair. At the judgment seat of Christ, before which we will all stand one day, for once in human history judgment will be fair.

Nearly every day we hear of the courts letting someone off, and we say to ourselves, "Where is the justice?" But God's justice is always fair. The question is, Will it occur here in this present life or in the life to come? The ancient Greek church father Chrysostom said it is in the life to come.

Paul said:

> For we must all appear before the judgment seat of Christ, that each one may receive what is due him for the things done while in the body, whether good or bad.
>
> —2 CORINTHIANS 5:10

> You, then, why do you judge your brother? Or why do you look down on your brother? For we will all stand before God's judgment seat.
>
> —ROMANS 14:10

"The Lord promises that equitable judgment will be administered."

On the other hand, God does deal with people in this present life, especially if they are saved. In 1 Corinthians 11:30, Paul says, "That is why many among you are weak and sick, and a number of you have fallen asleep." God doesn't always wait for the final judgment to begin disciplining His children.

Perhaps you have said, "Whew, I got away with that!" Perhaps God has closed His eyes to it. That *is* possible, since He has not always dealt with us after our sins nor rewarded us according to our iniquities (Ps. 103:10). On the other hand, it could be that God is so angry that He has decided to wait. Usually, the angrier He gets, the longer He waits.

God is not out to judge us because He enjoys punishing people. God is good, and God is on the side of the victim. God blesses the underdog, especially those who walk in an attitude of humility.

Everyone has been hurt or hurt another and God's grace and love is greater than it all. This book practically guides you through releasing those things that negatively impact your relationship with God, others and yourself. I won't sell this book, it has changed my life and shown me a freedom that I couldn't imagine.

—D. Higgins "ktmdirtchick"
Bucks County, PA

5

WHEN WE ARE RIGHT TO JUDGE

Why do you look at the speck of sawdust in your brother's eye and pay no attention to the plank in your own eye? How can you say to your brother, "Let me take the speck out of your eye," when all the time there is a plank in your own eye? You hypocrite, first take the plank out of your own eye, and then you will see clearly to remove the speck from your brother's eye.

—*Matthew 7:3–5*

After the strong language we encountered in Matthew 7:1, "Do not judge, or you too will be judged," it would be easy to conclude that there is *never* a situation in which we should make a judgment regarding another person. But this is not the case. When Jesus says, "First take the plank out of your own eye, and then you will see clearly to remove the speck from your brother's eye," He is not denying that there will be times in which we should help to remove the "specks" from the eyes of our brothers.

Sometimes it is absolutely right to warn others about someone's behavior. For example, the apostle John, who has so much to say about loving one another, warned about a troublemaker in the church. (See 3 John 9–10.) Paul reported that Demas had forsaken him because he "loved this world" and said that Alexander the metalworker had caused him "a great deal of harm" (2 Tim. 4:10, 14). But referring to all who had deserted him, Paul advised, "May it not be held against them" (v. 16).

When It Is Right to Correct Behavior

It is an injustice when certain people are at large who have done and can still do great harm to others. This is why a person who is raped should testify in court; it is why a person who threatens the unity of the church should be dealt with. But there are basic principles that must be followed in this type of judgment and that allow justice to be carried out without violating the spirit of the seven principles of total forgiveness.

Facing Our Own Faults First

Jesus introduced this matter of when we are right to judge with a question: "Why do you look at the speck of sawdust in your brother's eye and pay no attention to the plank in your own eye?" (Matt. 7:3). Since Jesus is addressing the church, it should not surprise us that so many of our quarrels come from within the family of God. He refers to your "brother's" eye—meaning one's spiritual brother or sister, not one's natural kin. This verse candidly shows how we tend to get upset over small issues (the "speck of dust") in another person's life and yet so easily overlook the big issues (the "plank") in our own lives. This lack of objectivity disqualifies us from being helpful. When we lose our objectivity, we render ourselves incapable of passing judgment on another person.

Faultfinding, then, is out of order. Jesus's rhetorical question forces us to confront our tendency to meddle over what gets our goat. The fault we see in someone else is what Jesus calls a "speck"—a little thing that annoys us. But the whole time we overlook our own very serious problems. Ironically, the cause of faultfinding, or meddling, is the plank in our own eye that we cannot see. *Plank* is Jesus's word for what is wrong with us; it is the sin in us, the evidence of our fallen nature. It is what makes us so eager to point the finger rather than to forgive.

"When we lose our objectivity, we render ourselves incapable of passing judgment on another person."

The planks in our eyes cause poor eyesight; they magnify the specks of dust in others while simultaneously blinding us to our own faults. The planks in our eyes focus on and enlarge the weaknesses in others so that they appear much worse than they really are; in actuality, it is our weaknesses that are in operation, simultaneously magnifying their faults and blinding us to our faults.

Jesus wants us to see that we have a serious problem when we are critical and point the finger. The act of faultfinding is worse than the fault we think we see in the other person. Before Jesus provides instruction about making a correction in another person,

He establishes the criterion for being qualified as a judge: we must look objectively at ourselves.

The question therefore follows: Is the faultfinding the plank in our eye, or is the plank some other sin in our life? Usually it is both.

Jesus elaborates on this when He asks, "How can you say to your brother, 'Let me take the speck out of your eye,' when all the time there is a plank in your own eye?" (Matt. 7:4). He is assuming we are rational, sensible people who would immediately see through the inconsistency of meddling in another's affairs. The assumption is this: if we have no plank in our own eye, it would not be unreasonable for us to offer help. But when we have a plank and still meddle, our fault is far worse than theirs. Meddling is always uninvited and almost always unwelcome.

> "The planks in our eyes cause poor eyesight; they magnify the specks of dust in others while simultaneously blinding us to our own faults."

How to Behave If Someone Criticizes Us

What if someone meddles in *your* life? How do you respond? Most of us find it hard to respond in a way that pleases God. First, He calls us to maintain a sweet spirit. Never forget: "A gentle answer turns away wrath, but a harsh word stirs up anger" (Prov. 15:1).

Second, we are to agree with them. Usually there is a little bit of truth in what a critic will say to us or about us. Even if you can't find a way to agree, you can always say, "I see what you mean."

Third, we should thank them. This will not only defuse their irritation, but it will also enable them to save face should they be up to no good. In addition, we will avoid making an enemy unnecessarily in the process.

What we must never do when being confronted is defend ourselves or try to impress them with how good or right we are. We must never seek to punish or get even or make them look bad. Ask them to pray for you! But do it in a noncombative manner, never sarcastically. Confess sincerely, "I need all the help I can get." The principles of total forgiveness should enable us to make friends, not lose them.

Jesus will not allow us to play God. He is the ultimate Judge, and we must be extremely careful not to trespass into His territory. The type of judgment that Jesus prohibits is *unfair criticism.* Jesus calls us hypocrites if we engage in this kind of judging: "You hypocrite, first take the plank out of your own eye, and then you will see clearly to remove the speck from your brother's eye" (Matt. 7:5).

Times When We Are Permitted to Judge

So, then, is Jesus telling us that we can be qualified to judge after all? Yes, sometimes we are. We have seen that the plank in our eye disqualifies us from judging since it blinds us to our own faults and magnifies the defects of others. On the other hand, if we are able to remove the plank from our own eyes, we are apparently set free to remove the speck from another's eye.

We must be careful here. Some people with absolutely no objectivity about themselves will claim to be qualified judges on the premise that they have no planks in their eyes! I have actually met people who can look at you with a straight face and claim their right to judge because they got rid of their plank years ago! And if you question them, *you* will be accused of judging!

> "The principles of total forgiveness should enable us to make friends, not lose them."

Are we to believe that Jesus is encouraging some of us to judge on the basis that we no longer have a plank in our eyes? If so, we are back to square one; we can all go back to pointing our fingers! This is arguably the most delicate question of this book. We all face unjust situations every day. How long are we to tolerate wrongdoing? People will take unfair advantage of others. And there may be a feeling in your bones that someone should speak out against the injustices. But because we are told to forgive and not to judge, it may not seem the right thing to do. Jesus even went so far as to say, "But I tell you, Do not resist an evil person. If someone strikes you on the right cheek, turn to him the other also" (Matt. 5:39).

So Surely We Can Never Judge?

According to Matthew 7:5, we can apparently judge another if we have no plank in our own eye. But who would be bold enough to say that he or she has no plank? I am certainly not that bold. Jeremiah 17:9 aptly describes my situation: "The heart is deceitful above all things and beyond cure. Who can understand it?"

When Paul says in Romans 7:18 that nothing good lives in him, I have to say, "That's me, too!" When he says in 1 Timothy 1:15, "Here is a trustworthy saying that deserves full acceptance: Christ Jesus came into the world to save sinners—of whom I am the worst," I am inclined to say, "That may have been true then, but now surely *I* am the worst."

If I must know that there is no plank in my eye before I can offer any sort of correction to or warning about an evil person, I have to say here and now that I am out of the picture! I will never be among those qualified to judge.

Matthew 7:5 is surely saying at least one of three things:

- ▷ No one ever gets rid of the plank; therefore, no one can ever judge.
- ▷ We can get rid of the plank and then—and only then—can we judge another person.
- ▷ The best situation occurs when one focuses on his or her *own* plank, and then self-effacingly offers correction to another in a way that will be most welcomed.

What is our Lord's purpose in these words? He wants to help us in the difficult situations we confront in life and bring a balance between a godly, forgiving spirit and an attitude of judgmentalism. It is possible to take the principle of total forgiveness to such an extent that we let all the rapists, child abusers, and murderers out of prison, allowing them to roam the streets and do more damage. You can allow "carnal Christians" to take over a church and destroy it if the principle of total forgiveness is not practiced with balance and common sense. (Yes, carnal Christians do exist! See 1 Corinthians 3:1ff.)

Jesus wants us to be honest with Him and with ourselves. Admit that you are unqualified as a judge as long as there is a plank in your eye. (And realize that we all have planks in our eyes at one time or another.)

Jesus also wants to promote humility. It would be the height of arrogance to claim we have completely gotten rid of our plank—arrogance tantamount to claiming to be without sin. But John said, "If we claim to be without sin, we deceive ourselves and the truth is not in us" (1 John 1:8).

Jesus wants us to move forward, past the offense into a lifestyle of forgiveness. Jesus also wants us to extend our help to others. But He never says we should not see what is very clearly there. Matthew 7:6, the very next verse in the Sermon on the Mount, tells us that we must be discriminating: "Do not give dogs what is sacred; do not throw your pearls to pigs. If you do, they may trample them under their feet, and then turn and tear you to pieces." In another place in the Gospel of Matthew, Jesus says:

> If your brother sins against you, go and show him his fault, just between the two of you. If he listens to you, you have won your brother over. But if he will not listen, take one or two others along, so that "every matter may be established by the testimony of two or three witnesses." If he refuses to listen to them, tell it to the church; and if he refuses to listen even to the church, treat him as you would a pagan or a tax collector.
>
> —Matthew 18:15–17

Perhaps the most relevant verse in the New Testament was written by the apostle Paul: "Brothers, if someone is caught in a sin, you who are spiritual should restore him gently. But watch yourself, or you also may be tempted" (Gal. 6:1).

In the Sermon on the Mount, our Lord is promoting honesty and humility, but He is also showing us what to do in certain situations where things have gone wrong—situations in which someone needs to speak out against sin or injustice, and it would be irresponsible not to do so. There is a way to truly help, however delicately, to remove the speck from our brother's or sister's eye *without meddling.*

> "Jesus wants us to move forward, past the offense into a lifestyle of forgiveness."

A closer look at Jesus's words shows us the order in which we should place our priorities: "First, take the plank out of your own eye." What we are required to do *first* is to admit that we have a plank and repent. If you and I want to help a person in need or speak up against an injustice, our first priority must be to get things right in our own hearts. This does not mean extracting a defect as a dentist removes a bad tooth (if only it were that simple!); it means to admit humbly and soberly our own weaknesses. That is the first step toward having self-objectivity.

Jesus is putting before us, quite ostensibly, a paradox. How are we ever to obliterate or remove the plank? We can't. Is this Jesus's tongue-in-cheek way of saying that we can never help another person with a fault? No. Is Jesus teaching sinless perfectionism that no one can truly attain? No.

> "If you and I want to help a person in need, or speak up against an injustice, our first priority must be to get things right in our own hearts."

No one can remove the plank in his or her own eye absolutely. If we could, we would be sinless and in no need of salvation! If Jesus were saying that the removal of the plank is possible, it would cause self-righteousness to flourish more than ever. People everywhere would claim to be qualified to point the finger.

Removing Our Plank in a Limited Way

It is, however, possible to remove the plank in a limited way. Galatians 6:1 tells us, "Brothers, if someone is caught in a sin, you who are spiritual should restore him gently. But watch yourself, or you also may be tempted."

Let us say I have found out that a brother in my church has fallen into the sin of adultery. He not only lusted (which would be adultery in the heart, according to Matthew 5:28), but he has also physically slept with a woman who was not his wife. I feel that someone must approach him about the situation. Am I qualified? In an absolute sense, no, because I am a sinner, too. As a matter of fact, without God's grace, I could very well see myself in his situation. But because I am *not* in an adulterous relationship, I have, in that particular area, removed the plank from my own eye. And the reason I am qualified to help is because I am not trying to find fault with him. I will let him know that I too am a sinner. I may not necessarily turn him around, but hopefully he will not resent my coming to him or see me as meddling. He will understand that I am concerned for his life and his spiritual state, not to mention the honor of God's name.

A few years ago two elders had the task of approaching a man in their church who was in an adulterous relationship. On their way to the man's home, one elder said to the other, "Do you believe that you too could fall into this sin?" The reply was, "No." The elder who asked the question then said, "You are not qualified to approach this man"—and the visit was canceled. The essential qualification for a spiritual confrontation is the attitude required by Paul in Galatians 6:1, one of humility and self-searching.

Here is a rule of thumb to follow: the one who is hardest on himself or herself will probably be the gentlest with others. Those who are most aware of their own weaknesses are most likely to be able to help others. The one who doesn't moralize but rather encourages others to become more like Christ is the one most qualified to engage in the ministry of reconciliation and restoration. The person who wants to help in a nonjudgmental way is aware of his own weaknesses. This person is more likely to succeed when others fail and to be welcomed when the meddler is rejected.

A qualified person will avoid becoming emotionally involved in the situation; he or she has no personal ax to grind. He is not agitated or inwardly churned up with bitterness or thoughts of revenge. His self-esteem is not connected to the situation.

> "The one who is hardest on himself or herself will probably be the gentlest with others."

When Jesus asks us to remove the plank from our own eyes, He is telling us that we should disqualify ourselves when we get upset with the one who has a speck! We are qualified to help another person only to the extent that we truly love and care for them. We cannot help if we are irritated with or annoyed by them.

For this reason it is often persons who are not personally connected to a situation who are best able to help. Such persons will be sympathetically detached—that is, like those trained to offer professional help, they will have sympathy for the people involved without allowing any prejudice or emotional involvement. Lawyers must sympathize with their clients but not become personally involved to the extent that they lose sleep. Ministers and doctors must be sympathetic toward the ones who call on their expertise, but they must never be so wound up that they cannot give a rational judgment of what is needed.

To be sympathetically detached means that you care about the person you want to help, but you are not fixated, or obsessed, with that person. A person who has a serious sexual weakness, for example, will almost certainly not be able to help the person who comes to them with the same problem. They could, in fact, actually make the situation worse!

Any counselor worth his salt will be both sympathetic and detached. Sometimes marital counseling is the only way to help a failing marriage, because the husband and wife may be neither sympathetic with the other nor detached; they are both likely up to their ears in emotional baggage. The impartiality of an outside counselor may be able to help a marriage in difficulty.

The person qualified to remove the speck of dust, then, is impartial. He or she will not moralize, hope to make the person feel guilty, or be governed by any personal interest. Their only consideration will be the honor of God's name.

Jesus never tells us how to remove the plank from our own eye, possibly because such a removal is not possible in the absolute sense. But paying sufficient attention to our own planks will keep us from pointing the finger at others or meddling in situations where we do not belong. We should continue to take care not to violate the words of Jesus that opened this discussion: "Do not judge, or you too will be judged" (Matt. 7:1).

When We *Can't* Help Another

To summarize, Jesus has provided some objective principles to follow when determining when it is right and wrong to judge.

You should rule yourself out when:

1. Your nose is out of joint because something or someone has gotten your goat. In other words, when you are churned up, stay out.

2. You are personally or emotionally involved. Even if an injustice has been committed, you should stay out of the situation—unless you have specifically been asked to testify or give your opinion.

3. Your desire is to punish or get even.

4. There is envy or jealousy in your heart.

5. Your own self-esteem is related.

When We *Can* Help Another

You are able to help when:

1. You are meeting a need. (To refresh your memory on this, here is the NEED acrostic I mentioned in chapter 4.)
    - ▷ **N**ecessary—Is it necessary to say this?
    - ▷ **E**ncourage—Will this encourage them? Will it make them feel better?
    - ▷ **E**dify—Will it edify? Will what you say build them up and make them stronger?
    - ▷ **D**ignify—Will it dignify that person? Jesus treated other people with a sense of dignity.
2. You would be irresponsible not to speak out. It is appropriate to get involved if you are in a strategic position to help.
3. You have been asked to step in by a responsible person who has no agenda.
4. You are utterly impartial and have no agitation or feeling of being annoyed.

5. Nothing matters to you more than the honor of God. Be careful! Many meddlers use this as their justification. One day you will find out whether it really was God's honor you cared about—or just your own!

Total Forgiveness truly "caught me by surprise" in regards to forgiving myself. Struggling with hurts and issues of the past, I began to realize my lack of self-forgiveness was a point of pride and self-righteousness that kept me in bondage and anguish. Releasing the past to God was the initial step for me to find peace and the true motivation to forgive others. To walk through the valley of forgiving ourselves is empowerment to stand on God's mountain of mercy.

—M.S.

6

THE ART OF FORGIVING AND FORGETTING

If we confess our sins, he is faithful and just and will forgive us our sins and purify us from all unrighteousness.

—1 John 1:9

First Corinthians 13, the great love chapter of the Bible, is a perfect demonstration of the cause and effect of total forgiveness. The apex of this wonderful passage is the phrase found in verse 5: love "keeps no record of wrongs." The Greek word that is translated as "no record" is *logizomai,* which means to not reckon or impute. This word is important to Paul's doctrine of justification by faith. For the person who believes, their faith is "credited" to them as righteousness (Rom. 4:5).

This is the same word used in 1 Corinthians 13:5. It is turned around in Romans 4:8, again using the same word: "Blessed is the man whose sin the Lord will never count against him." Therefore, *not* to reckon, impute, or "count" the wrongs of a loved one is to do for that person what God does for us, namely, choose not to recognize their sin. In God's sight our sin no longer exists. When we totally forgive someone, we too refuse to keep a record of their wrongs.

The Dangers of Keeping a Record of Wrongs

It must be clearly acknowledged that wrong was done, that evil took place. Total forgiveness obviously sees the evil but chooses to erase it. Before a grudge becomes lodged in the heart, the offense must be willfully forgotten. Resentment must not be given an opportunity to set in. The love described in 1 Corinthians 13 can only come by following a lifestyle of total forgiveness.

"When we totally forgive someone, we too refuse to keep a record of their wrongs."

Satan knows what we know. He hangs around day and night, waiting to exploit any weakness he can find in us. The single greatest weakness he loves to see is our inability to forgive. It was in the context of offering forgiveness that Paul said he was not ignorant of Satan's ways. (See 2 Corinthians 2:11.) Satan can take advantage of us through our bitterness—our refusal to let something drop and our insistence on dwelling on it. It is crucial that we rid our hearts of bitterness lest we hand the devil an invitation on a silver platter to enter our lives.

Why do we keep records, even mental ones, when others wrong us? To use them later. "I'll remember that," we say—and we are true to our word. And it usually comes up sooner rather than later. Although we may acknowledge with our minds the words of the Lord, "It is mine to avenge" (Rom. 12:19), we are really saying in our hearts, "God isn't doing His job." So we help God out by punishing that person who hurt us—whether it be a spouse, a relative, a church leader, an old schoolteacher, or an insensitive boss.

Letting Go of a Record of Wrongs

Love is a choice. It is an act of the will. Keeping a record of wrongs is also an act of the will—a choice *not* to love—and it is the more natural, easy choice for us to make.

Another key to letting go of the record of wrongs and achieving total forgiveness lies in the control of the tongue. The words that we say can cause the catastrophe to which James refers:

> Likewise the tongue is a small part of the body, but it makes great boasts. Consider what a great forest is set on fire by a small spark. The tongue also is a fire, a world of evil among the parts of the body. It corrupts the whole person, sets the whole course of his life on fire, and is itself set on fire by hell.
>
> —James 3:5–6

The irony is that, instead of "getting something off our chest," our words can cause an uncontrollable fire to erupt and incinerate what remains inside us. And instead of that fire subsiding, it doubles, intensifies, and gets a thousand times worse in the end. It is a satanic victory, ultimately traceable to our keeping a record of wrongs.

How does a person deal with their tongue? Two things, I believe, will help:

- When a person does wrong, refuse to point it out *to the person himself.*
- When a person does wrong, refuse to point it out *to others.*

If this were to become a more popular lifestyle, the number of records kept would plummet! By refusing to continually bring up the hurt in conversations, the record of that hurt would eventually disappear.

This principle also applies to imaginary conversations—those internal dialogues with yourself in which you can't get "what they did" off your mind. You may fantasize what you will say or do to them, or what you might tell other people about them. This conversation may go on and on—and hours and days may pass when you neither accomplish anything nor feel any better!

> "Keep no record of wrongs in your *thoughts,* and you will be less likely to expose such records by your *words.*"

One evening about eleven o'clock, as I was going to bed, I found myself having a conversation in my head about someone. I imagined I had the opportunity to spill the beans about this person. I pictured the scenario in great detail. I made myself look good and the other person look bad. But the Holy Spirit—

miraculously—got into the matter. I heard Him say to me, "You can get a victory right now if you refuse to think about clearing your name." Even though the conversation existed only in my mind, I realized that I had an opportunity to triumph—in my spirit! It was a pivotal moment, because it was as if it *were* real—and I refused to say anything at all about the person. I had achieved victory. A peace entered my heart, and I knew then and there that I must never again enter into those imaginary conversations—unless I refused to vindicate myself.

For those who find such conversations therapeutic, I would only remind you to let your thoughts be positive and wholesome; keep no record of wrongs in your *thoughts*, and you will be less likely to expose such records by your *words*.

When I am tempted to say something negative and I refuse to speak, I can often feel the release of the Holy Spirit within my heart. It is as if God says to me, "Well done." It is a very good feeling! After all, Jesus is touched with our weaknesses (Heb. 4:15), and He also lets us feel His joy when we overcome them! He rewards us with an incredible peace and the witness of the Spirit in our hearts.

Refusing to Keep a Record of Our Rights

Not keeping a record of wrongs is also a refusal to keep a record of the things you have done right. It is just as dishonoring to God's grace to keep a record of your rights as it is to keep a record of others' wrongs. Why? Because it is a form of self-exaltation. You are implicitly saying, "I told you so," in order to make someone else look bad. It takes spiritual maturity to refrain from saying, "I told you so."

More than a few people not only keep a record of wrongs, but they also have an even longer list of times when they have been right! We all want other people to know how right we have been. We want them to know that we said it first. It is amazing to me the advice that comes after the fact: "I knew it all along." "Do you see now how right I was?" "You should have listened to me." "I told you so!"

Love not only tears up the record of wrongs but also the list of rights. True forgivers destroy the record they might have used to vindicate themselves. If there is no record of rights lodged firmly in your head, you will not be able to refer to it later to prove how right you were. Forget what they did that was wrong, and forget what you did that was right. Paul said, "I do not even judge myself" (1 Cor. 4:3). I have often concluded that very few people really deserve the vindication they think they are entitled to. I can only say that if vindication is truly deserved, then that vindication will surely come, for God is just.

Jim Bakker's Experience of Letting Go of Wrongs

I recently watched an extraordinary edition of *Larry King Live* on CNN. Before the eyes of millions, Jim Bakker and Tammy Faye Messner (formerly Tammy Faye Bakker) appeared together on television for the first time in fifteen years. Jim Bakker, the television evangelist, had been sentenced to forty-five years in prison for something, it turned out, he had not done. He was initially found guilty of deliberately misleading his television viewers, encouraging them to send in money to buy homes that did not exist. He sat in prison for many years before he was vindicated. And in the meantime, his wife, Tammy Faye, divorced him and married his best friend, Roe Messner.

Eventually Jim was totally vindicated of the charges and was released from prison. Five years later, Jim married his present wife, Lori. Larry King invited the *four* of them to be on his TV program. What an interesting show it would turn out to be!

> "True forgivers destroy the record they might have used to vindicate themselves."

Each person had a story to tell—of deep, deep hurts and total forgiveness. Both Jim and Tammy, before Jim's imprisonment, had felt betrayed by the American minister who was almost entirely responsible for Jim being sentenced to prison. Both needed to forgive this minister. Tammy had to forgive Jim for his adulterous sexual encounter with a young woman—the episode that led to his downfall. Jim not only had to forgive the unjust witnesses and biased judge who had sentenced him unfairly, but also his wife for marrying his best friend while he was in prison. This is to say nothing about the hurts that the other two participants—Roe and Lori—had experienced.

Larry King asked Jim, "How did it feel?"

Jim replied, "We were in a situation that was unbelievable. I was to be in prison for forty-five years. At my age I would never have gotten out of prison before I died. And so I don't blame Tammy Faye for going on with her life."

Jim had not felt that way at first! But eventually he came to terms with the situation, totally forgave Tammy Faye, and fully appreciated her decision to marry Roe.

Jim continued, "Nelson Mandela says that he didn't look at prison as a down; he took it as an up. I suddenly found myself in prison for forty-five years—and my theology didn't allow for that at that time. It was like God had walked away from me. I know millions of people have gone through experiences saying, 'Why, God?' As I studied the Word of God and had more time to study the Bible, it was my faith in God that got me through. My faith was actually growing after five years. This experience was the greatest training seminary I ever went through, and my relationship with God became more intimate than ever."

Larry King then asked, "Are you saying, in a sense, in retrospect, it was good that you were in prison?"

> "When I began to study the words of Jesus Christ, I learned that He said if you don't forgive from the heart, forgiving everyone, you will not be forgiven."

Jim replied, "Absolutely, absolutely! I learned so much, and now that I am working in inner cities all over the world, I understand the people so much better. When I say I've been in prison, it's better than being an ordained minister. The people respond to me because they know I'm like them."

Larry then turned to Tammy and said, "You could help a lot of people because there's a lot of stories in the news now: the Guiliani story and the Clinton story. You were able to forgive and to overcome the worst thing a wife can go through. How were you able to do that?"

Tammy Faye answered, "Forgiveness is a choice. Our whole lives are made up of choices."

Larry then said to Tammy Faye, regarding Jim's affair, "You could have been bitter."

She replied, "I could have chosen to be bitter and hate him, or I could have chosen to forgive. It was very hard for me to forgive him; it was very hard. But . . . I was able to forgive him and understand what happened and go on."

Larry turned to Jim again: "And how did you feel about the forgiveness?"

Jim replied: "The Bible is so clear, and this is what I studied in prison. When I began to study the words of Jesus Christ, I learned that He said if you don't forgive from the heart, forgiving everyone, you will not be forgiven. Christ said, 'Blessed are the merciful for they shall obtain mercy.' I needed mercy; I needed forgiveness, so I wanted to give out to others what I myself needed."

Larry asked Jim, "Did you feel terrific she was able to forgive this?"

Jim answered, "Whether she forgave me or not, you know, I had to forgive her. I had to forgive everyone. I mean, everyone who goes through divorce, it's painful, and I took all the blame finally because I realized all the mistakes that I had made. I realized that I was the one who had the affair; I was the one who screwed up, and I had left her out there by herself to literally face dying without a husband."

Larry turned again to Tammy, "So you're friendly now. How do you explain that?"

Tammy replied, "I like this man [Jim]; he's a really nice man. We were married for thirty years, and we've had wonderful memories together. We had two awesome kids together, and I genuinely like him."

Larry asked Jim if he ever prayed for Roe. He answered, "Absolutely I pray for Roe. I had to really forgive Roe for marrying my wife at that point in prison. I mean, you have to forgive. I'm in prison and God was dealing with me to forgive everybody. You can't just forgive; you've got to pray for God to bless your enemies."

Larry responded, "It doesn't make it easy, does it?"

Jim then said, "I had to come to the point where I had to literally tell God—Roe's one of the greatest builders in the world—and I had to say to God, 'If, God, You want me to ever build something again, I would build it with Roe Messner.' And I had come to that point where I could say, 'God, Your will be done, not my will be done.'"

Larry then looked at all four persons before him and asked, "There's no jealousy in this room?"

The unanimous answer: "No."

"Do you say that you're all friends?" asked Larry.

The unanimous answer: "Yes."

"How do you explain that?" asked Larry King.

Jim Bakker stepped in. "Only God can help people truly

forgive and go on. In the Book of Colossians it talks about that. Because of what Christ did, we are pure; we are without judgment on ourselves. When I first went to prison, I was even questioning, 'Where, God? Where are You?' But as I went through the months of studying the Word of God, I realized that prison was God's plan for me. God was saying, 'I want you to come aside and be with Me.' Everyone in the Bible, from Genesis to Revelation, has either been in a pit or a prison or the backside of the desert. They've all been through bad things. So bad things do happen to people—they happened to all the great men of God."

Larry King then concluded the interview by echoing what millions watching must have thought: "I'm amazed," he said.[1]

> "Forgiving oneself means to experience the love that keeps no record of our *own* wrongs."

Jim Bakker had been vindicated. A law professor at Fordham University stepped in out of the blue and took on Jim's case. He showed convincingly that Bakker was totally innocent of the charges of fraud, and after five years in prison Jim was released. He went on to live in solitude for a long while on a farm in North Carolina. His biggest problem, he says, was forgiving himself. He never believed for a moment he was guilty of financial dishonesty, but he knew he had erred in at least two areas: his sexual affair and his prosperity teaching—that God will make anyone prosperous who follows certain formulas. He knew he had been wrong. How could he forgive himself?

Forgiving Ourselves

Forgiving oneself means to experience the love that keeps no record of our *own* wrongs. This love is a choice, as we have seen, and to cross over to the place where we choose to forgive ourselves is no small step.

It is one thing to have this breakthrough regarding others—totally forgiving them and destroying the record of their wrongs; it is quite another to experience the greater breakthrough—total forgiveness of ourselves.

So many Christians say, "I can forgive others, but how can I ever forget what I have done? I know God forgives me, but I can't forgive myself."

We must remember that forgiving ourselves is also a lifelong commitment. In precisely the same way that I must forgive others every single day—which is why I read Luke 6:37 daily—I must also forgive myself.

Forgiving others is a lifelong commitment because:

- We are so often made to relive the wrong committed against us.
- We may feel irked that the offender is getting away with it—forever.
- Satan moves in to exploit our weakness in this area.

This is why we must *renew* our commitment to forgive each and every day—and be sure we haven't pasted together those torn-up bits of paper we once used to record the wrongs done to us.

Forgiving ourselves is also a daily process. We may wake up each day with the awareness of past mistakes and failures—and fervently wish that we could turn the clock back and start all over. We may have feelings of guilt—or *pseudoguilt*, if our sins have been placed under the blood of Christ. But the enemy, the devil, loves to move in and take advantage of our thoughts. That is why forgiving ourselves is as important as forgiving an enemy.

Forgiving yourself may bring about the breakthrough you have been looking for. It could set you free in ways you have never before experienced. This is because we have been afraid to forgive ourselves. We cling to fear as if it were a thing of value. The truth is, this kind of fear is no friend but rather a fierce enemy. The very breath of Satan is behind the fear of forgiving ourselves.

> "Forgiving yourself may bring about the breakthrough you have been looking for. It could set you free in ways you have never before experienced."

Jesus knows that many of us have this problem. This is a further reason Jesus turned up unexpectedly after His resurrection where, behind closed doors, the disciples were assembled both in terror and in guilt. Jesus not only wanted them to know they were totally forgiven; He also wanted them to forgive themselves. Instead of reminding them of what they had done, He spoke to them as if nothing had happened. He said, "As the Father has sent me, I am sending you" (John 20:21). This gave them dignity. It showed them that nothing had occurred that would change Jesus's plans and strategy for them. He had already sent a signal to Peter, who had denied knowing Jesus, through the angel who said, "But go, tell his disciples and Peter, 'He is going ahead of you into Galilee. There you will see him, just as he told you'" (Mark 16:7). And yet all of them had "deserted him and fled" (Matt. 26:56). After His crucifixion, they felt utterly unworthy. And then the risen Lord showed up and assured them of a future ministry!

> "When we are emptied of all self-righteousness and pride, we enable God to move in and through us."

I have often thought that one of the reasons Peter was so effective on the Day of Pentecost is that he was keenly aware of having been forgiven. He knew full well that, just a few weeks before, he had denied Jesus to a little servant girl! He would never forget the look on Jesus's face when the rooster crowed, and Peter "went outside and wept bitterly" (Luke 22:61–62). It was a real antidote to self-righteousness! When Peter preached to his fellow Jews on the Day of Pentecost, there was no trace of smugness or condescension. Knowing he was a forgiven sinner also kept him from usurping God's glory on that day. God alone received the glory for those three thousand conversions.

I well remember one Sunday morning just before I was to preach at the eleven o'clock service. I had an argument with my wife, Louise. I should never have done it, but I stormed out, slamming the door in her face. Before I knew it, I was bowing my head on the upper platform at Westminster Chapel before several hundred people. I don't know what they were thinking, but I know what *I* was thinking: "I should not be here. I have no right to be here. Lord, how on earth could You use me today? I am not fit to be in this pulpit." It was too late to send a note to Louise saying, "I'm sorry." There was no way to resolve the situation at that time. I could only ask God for mercy and try my best to forgive myself. I assumed I was about to deliver the biggest flop of a sermon in the history of Westminster Chapel. Never in my life had I felt so unworthy. But when I stood up to preach, I was not prepared for the help I got. God simply undergirded me and enabled me to preach as well as I ever had!

That is partly why I think Peter was so successful on the Day of Pentecost. When we are emptied of all self-righteousness and pride, we enable God to move in and through us.

Signs That We Haven't Forgiven Ourselves

If we feel guilty, blame ourselves, and find that we cannot function normally—even though we have confessed our sins to God—it indicates that we haven't yet totally forgiven ourselves. It means that we are still hanging on to guilt that God has washed away; we are refusing to enjoy what God has freely given us. First John 1:9 either is true or it isn't: "If we confess our sins, he is faithful and just and will forgive us our sins and purify us from all unrighteousness." If we have confessed our sins, we must take this promise with both hands and forgive ourselves—which is precisely what God wants us to do.

The person who hasn't forgiven himself is an unhappy person—and is usually unable to forgive others. Thus, my not forgiving myself will often backfire, and I will struggle to forgive others. Or my not forgiving others may result in a sense of shame that causes unforgiveness of myself. The irony is, the degree to which we forgive others will often be the degree to which we forgive ourselves; the degree to which we set ourselves free will often be the degree to which we forgive others.

It is like the age-old question: Which comes first—the chicken or the egg? It is sometimes almost impossible to say which comes first—forgiving others so you will be able to forgive yourself, or forgiving yourself so you will be able to forgive others. But it is not *total* forgiveness until both are equally true.

Why Can't We Forgive Ourselves?

What causes our inability to forgive ourselves? At the end of the day, why don't we forgive ourselves?

Anger

We may be angry with ourselves. Look back at the Old Testament story of Joseph that we examined in chapter 2. As a type of Christ, Joseph said to his brothers, "And now, do not be distressed and do not be angry with yourselves for selling me here, because it was to save lives that God sent me ahead of you" (Gen. 45:5). These brothers were beginning to get the message that Joseph had forgiven them. But Joseph knew they would struggle with forgiving themselves. One of the proofs that Joseph had totally forgiven them was that he didn't want them to be angry with themselves.

That is the way God forgives. He doesn't want us to be angry with ourselves for our sins. Jesus forgives us in the same exact manner in which Joseph forgave his brothers; just as Joseph did not want his brothers to be angry with themselves, so Jesus does not want us to be angry with ourselves.

Not forgiving ourselves is self-hatred; it is being angry with ourselves. Joseph's brothers had hated themselves for twenty-two years for selling Joseph into slavery. They could not turn the clock back or take back what they had done. They could not get a second chance.

> "It is almost impossible to say which comes first—forgiving others so you will be able to forgive yourself, or forgiving yourself so you will be able to forgive others. But it is *not* total forgiveness until both are equally true."

Jesus says to you and me, "Don't be angry with yourself." Peter was none the worse for his denial of Jesus. He felt ashamed, yes. But his pride and ego were diminished, and I suspect he was easier to live with after that!

I remember talking with a minister who told me about a sexual affair of another preacher. He went on and on about how disgusting and reprehensible this man's behavior had been. He wanted my opinion on what should be done. I said, "Don't tell anyone else; just pray for this man."

"Really?" asked this minister, who wanted me to enter into his feeling of disgust.

I repeated, "Say nothing."

"Really?" this man said again.

"Yes," I said. "It could happen to you if you were put in the same situation."

I remember feeling a little uncomfortable with that man. I said to myself, "If, God forbid, I ever fall into sin in any shape or fashion, this is the last man I would ever tell."

> "God can take your sinful past and make it work together for your good—so brilliantly and beautifully that you will be tempted to say that, that is the way it was supposed to be!"

But that is not the end of the story. A few years later the same minister came to me with a problem. He had become attracted to a woman in his congregation. I immediately recalled the previous conversation I had had with him—but I said nothing about it. I simply urged this man to break the relationship off—utterly and immediately. It ended, thankfully, and the man continued to preach. He confessed his sin to God and received forgiveness. But there is more: after this incident, his preaching became more tender and his general spirit was more gracious than self-righteous.

We should not need to have an affair—or even come close—in order to overcome the sin of pride and self-righteousness. I have known some hypocritical Christians who became even more self-righteous after falling into sin; they began to justify all they had done. The answer to self-righteousness is not found in an opportunity to sin. Don't be a fool. But what is true is this: God can take your sinful past and make it work together for your good—so brilliantly and beautifully that you will be tempted to say that, that is the way it was supposed to be!

Some Christians who can't forgive themselves are, underneath it all, angry with themselves. But God can begin today to cause all that happened to fit into a pattern for good. Begin to forgive yourself. And don't feel guilty about doing so! God says, "Take your forgiveness and don't look back." God will take the wasted years and restore them to good before it is all over. It is just as God promised in the Book of Joel: "I will repay you for the years the locusts have eaten" (Joel 2:25).

In some cases it is fear more than anger that is a barrier to our forgiving ourselves. Regret over the past leads to guilt, and guilt can lead to fear: the fear of missing "what might have been" or the fear that what has happened cannot possibly turn out for good.

True guilt and pseudoguilt

There are two kinds of guilt most of us will struggle with: true guilt (a result of our sin against God) and pseudoguilt (when there is no sin in our lives). When we have sinned—as Joseph's brothers did and as Peter and the disciples did—we must confess it to God (1 John 1:9). The blood of Jesus takes care of true guilt by doing two basic things:

- It washes away our sin—as though it never had existed.
- It perfectly satisfies God's eternal justice.

God is looking only to His Son's precious blood for satisfaction. Any chastening or discipline that comes from our Father is not adding to Jesus's blood. He is not getting even with us; He "got even" at the cross. The Greek word that translates as "chastening" or "discipline" in Hebrews 12:6 means "enforced learning." When God teaches us a lesson, He makes sure we learn it! Whereas discipline is necessary because we are sinners, it does not follow that God is looking for more satisfaction for His just nature. Sin that has been confessed to God is totally forgiven by Him, and any guilt we feel after that is pseudoguilt.

There are also two kinds of this false guilt:

- ▹ When sin was never involved in the first place
- ▹ When sin has been forgiven

Pseudoguilt—though it is false—is also very real; that is, we feel keenly guilty. But it is called pseudoguilt because, when it is thought through, there is *no good reason* for feeling guilty.

Take, for example, a person who is driving a car when a child runs out into the street at the last second and is struck down. The guilt can be overwhelming, but there was no sin. It doesn't need to be confessed to God.

Another example of false guilt is missing out on an opportunity. I have a friend in Florida who had a chance to buy a property many years ago for five thousand dollars. He turned down the offer. Today that property is worth over a million dollars. He feels guilty that he didn't use his money more wisely, but this is not true guilt.

The list of ways pseudoguilt can adversely affect our lives is endless. We can become weighed down over something that, in actuality, had nothing to do with us: not speaking to a person when you didn't even see them, not answering a letter you never received, and so on. These are not necessarily sins, but they can make us feel guilty.

> "Sin that has been confessed to God is totally forgiven by Him, and any guilt we feel after that is pseudoguilt."

The other kind of pseudoguilt is when you have confessed your sins—you may have even repented deeply—but you don't feel forgiven. Once you have acknowledged your sin, you should accept your forgiveness and leave the rest in God's hands.

Over the years I have developed a sense of failure as a father. Children spell *love* T-I-M-E. I wish I had given more time to TR and Melissa in those early years at Westminster Chapel. I now understand that putting them first—not my church or sermon preparation—would have resulted in the Chapel carrying on just as well, if not better. But it's too late now. For me to continue to feel guilty over this is not pleasing to God, because He has already totally forgiven me. He wants me to accept my forgiveness and let Him restore the years the locusts have eaten. If I let myself dwell on my failure, I am giving in to pseudoguilt—and sinning as I do it, because I am dignifying unbelief. I must keep destroying the record of my wrongs—every day.

Not forgiving ourselves is a subtle way of competing with Christ's atonement. God has already punished Jesus for what we did. (See 2 Corinthians 5:17.) When we don't accept our own forgiveness, we are punishing ourselves. Instead of accepting

Jesus's sacrifice, I want to punish myself for my failures. This competes with Christ's finest hour.

Fear and not forgiving ourselves

Fear, then, is one of the main reasons we do not forgive ourselves. He or she who fears has not been made perfect in love, and fear "has to do with punishment" (1 John 4:18). But Paul tells us, "For you did not receive a spirit that makes you a slave again to fear, but you received the Spirit of sonship. And by him we cry, '*Abba*, Father'" (Rom. 8:15, emphasis added). Paul said to Timothy, "For God did not give us a spirit of timidity, but a spirit of power, of love and of self-discipline" (2 Tim. 1:7).

> "Let the past be past—at last."

Recognizing that fear—and punishing ourselves for our mistakes—displeases God should result in an ever-increasing sadness for this self-loathing spirit. We are required to walk away from our past folly. And when we are tempted to look back, we must obey that sign, "No trespassing allowed."

My wife was greatly blessed by the ministry of Rodney Howard-Browne, especially when she attended a week of his services in Lakeland, Florida, in January 1995. But it was not only Rodney's ministry that helped Louise; it was also the music ministry of Janny Grein and her song "Stronger Than Before." Louise remembers Janny shouting out the words: "Let the past be past—at last."

God speaks those words to us. Let the past be past at last. Forgive yourself as well as those who have damaged you.

Pride, self-righteousness, and self-pity

At the end of the day, our unforgiveness of ourselves may be traceable to pride. That is what is ultimately at work when we compete with the blood of Christ. We, in our arrogance and self-righteousness, cannot bear the Lord doing everything for us so graciously, so we think we must help Him out a bit. It is an abominable way to think. Our pride must be eclipsed by humility; we must let God be God and the blood of Christ do what it in fact did: remove our guilt and satisfy God's sense of justice.

Just as fear and pride are like identical twins, so are self-righteousness and self-pity. We feel sorry for ourselves and show it by not forgiving ourselves. That is why pseudoguilt can develop into very real and heinous guilt before God. It is false guilt, since God says, "You're not guilty." We make it into real guilt when we in effect reply, "Yes, I am."

The bottom line is this: not forgiving ourselves is wrong and dishonoring to God.

At this point you may be saying, "I agree. I know not forgiving myself is wrong. I just can't help it." What can be done to help you forgive yourself if you truly want to?

Understanding guilt

The ability to forgive ourselves comes partly from understanding guilt. Guilt is, at heart, a feeling that one is to blame. For example, when you blame others, you have kept a record of their wrongs. But when you blame yourself, you have kept a record of your own wrongs. The Holy Spirit shows us our sin; the initial work of the Spirit according to John 16:8 is that He convicts of sin. When Isaiah saw the glory of the Lord, he was convicted of his sin. (See Isaiah 6:1–5.) When we walk in the light we know the blood cleanses us of sin, but walking in the light also reveals sin in us that we may not have seen before (1 John 1:7–8).

But the sense of guilt God instigates is temporary.

> For his anger lasts only a moment, but his favor lasts a lifetime; weeping may remain for a night, but rejoicing comes in the morning.
>
> —Psalm 30:5

God only uses guilt to get our attention. When we say, "I'm sorry," and mean it, that's enough for God. He doesn't beat us black and blue and require us to go on a thirty-day fast to supplement Christ's atonement. He convicts us of sin to get our attention, but having done that, He wants us to move forward.

Understanding grace

The ability to forgive ourselves therefore extends from an understanding of grace. Grace is undeserved favor. Mercy is not getting what we do deserve (justice); grace is getting what we don't deserve (total forgiveness). Grace isn't grace if we have to be good enough for it to apply to us.

Peter *knew* what he had done and knew he was forgiven. David *knew* what he had done and pleaded for God's mercy. (See Psalm 51.) Grace is accepting what we don't deserve. It may seem unfair when we have been so horrible. We have let God down; we have let others down.

> "We must let God be God and the blood of Christ do what it in fact did: remove our guilt and satisfy God's sense of justice."

But it *is* fair, says John: "If we confess our sins, he is faithful and just and will forgive us our sins and purify us from all unrighteousness" (1 John 1:9). The blood of Jesus did a wonderful job. God is not looking for further satisfaction. We forgive ourselves to the degree we really do believe that!

All accusations regarding confessed sin come from the devil. When you know you have applied 1 John 1:9, and you still sense an accusing voice over that past failure, mark it down. That voice did not come from your heavenly Father. It did not come from Jesus. It did not come from the Holy Spirit. It came from your enemy, the devil, who works either as a roaring lion to scare or as an angel of light to deceive—or both (1 Pet. 5:8; 2 Cor. 11:14). Never forget, perfect love drives out fear (1 John 4:18).

Let the Past Be Past

The sweet consequence of not keeping a record of all wrongs is that we let go of the past and its effect on the present. We cast our care on God and rely on Him to restore the wasted years and to cause everything to turn out for good. We find ourselves, almost miraculously, accepting ourselves as we are (just as God does) with all our failures (just as God does), knowing all the while our potential to make more mistakes. God never becomes disillusioned with us; He loves us and knows us inside out.

> Grace isn't grace if we have to be good enough for it to apply to us.

Moses had a past. He was a murderer. (See Exodus 2:11–12.) But years later he would proclaim the eighth commandment: you shall not murder (Exod. 20:13). David had a past, but he also had a future after his shame: "Then I will teach transgressors your ways, and sinners will turn back to you," he wrote (Ps. 51:13). Jonah deliberately ran from God, but he was still used in an astonishing revival (Jon. 3). Peter's disgrace—denying Jesus—did not abort God's plans for him. But all these men had to forgive themselves before they could move into the ministry God had planned for them.

Can you do that? Having forgiven others, it is time to forgive yourself. That is exactly what God wants of you and me. It is long overdue: let the past be past—at last.

Thank you so much for living and writing *Total Forgiveness.* I knew that I had to read your book. My wife of nearly sixteen years got involved in an affair with a pastor of a local church. She asked me to move out. I took the book with me. I knew I'd need it.

It challenged me with such vigor, and I couldn't ignore the message. I knew that I was faced with only one choice—I had to forgive them and myself totally. The experience was wonderful. A weight was lifted off of me as I began on a new path of working through my own problems, changing the things that I could and leaving the other issues—like the state of their hearts—in God's hands.

I forgive them over and over again. I refuse to let Satan get a foothold in my life by using my own anger against me. I give glory to God, because He prepared my heart before I ever knew of a problem so that when the news broke, I was firmly in His hands.

—S.G.

7

HOW TO FORGIVE—TOTALLY

But I tell you: Love your enemies and pray for those who persecute you.
—Matthew 5:44

NOT EVERYONE WE must forgive is an enemy. There are those we must forgive who either do not know they have hurt us or, if they do, would never have done so intentionally. But we must forgive anyone for whom we feel anger, because it is we, not they, who are in need of healing. That is why total forgiveness—in a sense—becomes a selfish thing. As Jim Bakker said, "Christ said, 'Blessed are the merciful for they will be shown mercy.' I needed mercy, I needed forgiveness, so I wanted to give out to others what I needed."[1]

Forgiving Those Who Are Not Enemies

Some of the people I have had to forgive the most were not my enemies at all. By this I mean that they were not trying to bring me down or hurt me. They were people I had hoped would help me.

On one occasion I asked an old friend to write a commendation for a book I had written. He refused, partly because there wasn't enough in it he agreed with and partly because I was gaining a reputation for mixing with people of whom he didn't approve. This hurt. He was no enemy, but I had to forgive him. I have had to forgive those who felt a need to distance themselves from me because I don't echo their "party line." I have had to forgive those who no longer need me as they once did. All of these things hurt. The irony is that it is sometimes harder to forgive those who are not enemies, but who have hurt you deeply, than it is to forgive one who is indeed an enemy.

"The greater the hurt, the greater the blessing that will come with forgiveness."

I do believe I have had some enemies in my life—people who were not only opposed to me and my teaching but who also actively sought to bring me down and destroy my reputation. I have had to forgive them—totally—and I believe by the grace of God that I truly have.

The greater the hurt, the greater the blessing that will come with forgiveness. The chief motivation to forgive is not only the promise of mercy that will be extended to us, but also the greater reward that is promised—whether it be bestowed here below or in heaven. Jesus confirmed this when He spoke of the ultimate Beatitude:

> Blessed are you when people insult you, persecute you and falsely say all kinds of evil against you because of me. Rejoice and be glad, because great is your reward in heaven, for in the same way they persecuted the prophets who were before you.
>
> —Matthew 5:11–12

If you have a real, relentless, genuine enemy—someone who is not a figment of your anxiety or imagination—you should see yourself as sitting on a mine of twenty-four carat gold. Not everybody is that blessed! But if you have been blessed in that way, take it with both hands. You should take this person's picture, enlarge it, frame it, and thank God every time you look at it. Your enemy, should you handle him or her correctly, could turn out to be the best thing that ever happened to you.

As I was preparing to write this very chapter, I related to my wife the incident that led to my having to forgive those who hurt me many years ago. I told her that it was "the best thing that ever happened to me." Perhaps that is a *slight* exaggeration when I think of all the other wonderful things that have happened to me—my conversion and my marriage to Louise being the top two. But that is often the way I feel; I wouldn't take *anything* in exchange for the devastating incident that led Josif Tson to say to me, "RT, you must totally forgive them."

> When through the deep waters
> I call thee to go,
> The rivers of sorrow
> Shall not overflow;
> For I will be with thee
> Thy trials to bless,

And sanctify to thee
Thy deepest distress.[2]

What Do We Mean by Having an Enemy?

What is an enemy? It is a person who either wants to harm you or who would say something about you so as to call your credibility or integrity into question. They would rejoice at your downfall or lack of success. They would not pray that God would bless you and prosper you, but instead they would sincerely hope that God would bring you down.

An enemy is a person who hates you although they would never admit to the word *hate*. I say that because, should your enemy be a Christian, they know it is wrong to hate. So they will use any other word or phrase: "loathe," "despise," "I just can't stand them," "They make me sick," "I can't stand the sight of them." In other words, they just don't like you, and they will show it one way or another, sooner or later.

> "When you totally forgive your enemy, you have crossed over into the supernatural realm."

An enemy is also a person who will take unfair advantage of you; they will "despitefully use you" (Matt. 5:44, KJV). They will walk all over you. If they know you place vengeance in God's hands rather than your own, instead of respecting this they will exploit it all the more—knowing you will not retaliate. Sometimes a Christian will be unscrupulous in business with another believer, because they know this particular Christian would never take them to court. (See 1 Corinthians 6:1–8.) They may say libelous things in print, because they know you will not sue.

An enemy will often persecute you. The Greek word for "persecute" simply means "to follow" or "to pursue." Enemies will pursue you, because they are obsessed with you. King Saul became jealous of David, because he had become more popular, and King Saul was more worried about the threat of David's anointing than he was of Israel's archenemy—the Philistines! Saul pursued David, but he never succeeded in killing him.

The persecutor's main tactic is to discredit you. They will speak badly about you to your boss, keeping you from getting that promotion or raise in pay; they will tell your friends about any indiscretions they might perceive in your life; they will go out of their way to keep you from succeeding and from being admired by the people in the office or at church. What is more, if they are Christians they may deceive themselves into thinking that they are doing it for God and His glory! "They will put you out of the synagogue; in fact, a time is coming when anyone who kills you will think he is offering a service to God" (John 16:2). Persecutors don't kill with the sword or a gun; they do it with the tongue or pen. Perhaps sometimes you wish they would just physically kill you and get it over with!

The Blessing of Having an Enemy

When you know that a person is obsessed with you and is out to discredit you, you are very, very blessed indeed. This doesn't happen to everyone. You are chosen, for behind your enemy is the hand of God. God has raised up your enemy—possibly just for you! King Saul's pursuit of David was the best thing that could have happened to David at the time. It was a part—a most vital part—of David's preparation to become king. He had the anointing (1 Sam. 16:13) without the crown, and God was ensuring that when the day came for him to wear the crown, he would be ready. Remember the quote of Dr. Martyn Lloyd-Jones: "The worst thing that can happen to a man is to succeed before he is ready." God did David a very special favor: He raised up Saul to keep him on his toes, to teach him to be sensitive to the Spirit (1 Sam. 24:5), and to teach him total forgiveness. Saul was David's passport to a greater anointing.

Totally Forgiving Our Enemies

When you totally forgive your enemy, you have crossed over into the supernatural realm. Perhaps you are like me and wish you could excel in all the gifts of the Spirit; you wish you could have a hand in signs and wonders; you'd love to see your usefulness intensified and extended by a double anointing. The gifts are *supernatural*; that is, they are above and beyond the natural order of things. There is no natural explanation for the truly miraculous. But if you and I totally forgive one who is truly an enemy, believe me, we have just crossed over into the realm of the supernatural.

You may not speak in tongues; you may not have raised a person from the dead. But when you totally forgive an authentic enemy, you are *there*: you have made it into the big leagues.

I believe we are talking about the highest level of spirituality that exists. This is as good as it gets. Totally forgiving an enemy is as spectacular as any miracle. No one may even know, though.

You quietly intercede for them in solitude. Only God, the angels, and the devil know.

We are talking about a feat greater than climbing Mount Everest, for totally forgiving an enemy is to climb the spiritual Everest. It means the highest watermark in anyone's spiritual pilgrimage.

> "Whether your enemy is temporary or a "life sentence," never forget that God is at the bottom of it all."

And yet it is within reach of any of us. No high connections in government, business, or society are required. No particular cultural background is needed. No university education is needed. A high level of intelligence is not required. You and I can do something exceedingly rare: forgive an enemy (if we have one). Loving an enemy defies natural explanation.

It begins with having sufficient motivation. I am literally seeking to motivate you in these lines to do what very few do—but which all *can* do: totally forgive anyone who has hurt you. And the blessing is beyond words to describe.

Why Do I Have Enemies?

When Jesus said, "Love your enemies," He assumed that we would have one or more, and most people do. Sadly, many, if not most, of them will be from within the community of faith. Certainly Jesus assumed this, and nothing has really changed. Much persecution comes from those who claim to believe in God as much as you do. And yet the issues between you may not be theological. Your enemy simply may *not like you!*

The origin of such enmity may be explained almost entirely in terms of the flesh. For example, your enemy may just not be able to cope with your being the way you are or with your being on a particular side of a certain question or issue. It is usually no fault of your own.

They could be angry with God for blessing you or for putting you where you are. You have that prestigious job. It pays well. You are admired by your boss and the people in the office. God has blessed you with certain talents and gifts. There will always be someone who will be jealous and seek to bring you down. If you have been blessed with a good reputation, do not be surprised if someone resents it. Unfortunately, your enemy doesn't know that he or she is probably actually angry with God.

Whereas a good case can be made that the motivation behind your enemy is the devil (John 13:2) as well as the sinful flesh, the ultimate reason you and I have an enemy is that it fits *God's purpose*. Why? It is what we need. David needed an enemy. So do you and I. It helps to humble us lest we take ourselves too seriously. An enemy shows us what we are like. Frequently God will allow an enemy to make a broadside attack on us—and then God appears to desert us. He did this with Hezekiah in order to test him and see what was in his heart (2 Chron. 32:31). In our case, God often raises up an enemy to see if we really want to be like Jesus.

So don't be angry with your enemy! It is God who is at work on your heart! "But doesn't God want me to succeed?" you might ask.

Yes, if your success is His idea: "Delight yourself in the Lord and he will give you the desires of your heart" (Ps. 37:4). If your goals stay the same the longer you love God, it may be a good sign you will reach them—in His timing. God will exalt you in due time (1 Pet. 5:6). God designs an enemy to keep us on our toes, but also on our knees. He is sovereign. He knows exactly what we need. He will keep our enemy alive and well as long as we need them. Whether your enemy is temporary or a "life sentence," never forget that God is at the bottom of it all.

> "The paradox in total forgiveness is that it simultaneously involves selfishness and unselfishness."

I was recently preaching in Northern Ireland where a minister came up to me after the service and asked, "Can your wife be your enemy?" That question took me by surprise!

I replied, "Yes." I believe that in a marriage a husband and wife can develop such a dislike for each other that the only way forward for that marriage is Jesus's teaching on total forgiveness. Everything that can be said about an enemy in general may describe a husband or wife in particular. The only way to heal the situation is to forgive. Totally.

Your enemy's objective is to punish you in any way he can. To put you in your place. To keep you checked. They think that if they don't do this, then it won't be done. They may even feel that they are an instrument God will use to put you in your place. But while their motives may be carnal, God's purpose is for our sanctification.

Loving Our Enemies

Jesus puts to us the greatest challenge that ever was—a greater challenge to the human spirit than science faced in putting a man on the moon. It is, simply, to love your enemy. Jesus uses the word *agape*, as Paul did in 1 Corinthians 13. It is not *eros* (physical or sexual love), nor is it *phileo* (brotherly love). *Agape* is *selfless concern for others.* It is self-giving love. Agape is not necessarily affection. You may love (agape) a person and not like them. You may love a person and not want to spend a holiday with them. You can love a person and act selfishly toward them.

This challenge can be almost overwhelming. Jesus instructs us to overcome our enemy, not by showing everybody how wrong he or she was or by matching their hatred with ours, but by loving them.

This brings us back to the matter of choice. Love is not what you feel. Forgiving is not doing what comes naturally. It is often said, "You can't help what you feel." We therefore ask, does the choice to love involve repressing or denying our feelings? No. Repression is almost never a good thing to do. But love is a conscious choice to forgive—even if you don't feel like it! If you wait until you feel like it, you probably never will forgive. You must do it because it is right, because of a choice you have made that is not based on your feelings.

Nelson Mandela has been asked many times how he emerged from all those years in prison without being bitter. His reply is simple: "Bitterness only hurts oneself." Oddly, many who are bitter fully realize this, yet they still can't forgive. They rationally understand that bitterness is self-impoverishing, but they continue to harbor it. How did Nelson Mandela overcome his feelings? The answer can be found in his own words: "If you hate, you will give them your heart and mind. Don't give those two things away."

The paradox in total forgiveness is that it simultaneously involves selfishness and unselfishness. It is selfish in that you do not want to hurt yourself by holding on to bitterness, and it is unselfish in that you commit yourself to the well-being of your enemy! You could almost say that total forgiveness is both extreme selfishness and extreme unselfishness. You are looking out for your own interests when you totally forgive, but you are also totally setting your offender free.

Even the non-Christian understands the benefits of forgiveness in a physical and emotional sense. This surely leaves all of us without excuse. If a non-Christian is able to forgive others, how much more should the Christian follow a lifestyle of forgiveness? We are the ones who have been warned by Jesus:

> For if you forgive men when they sin against you, your heavenly Father will also forgive you. But if you do not forgive men their sins, your Father will not forgive your sin.
>
> —Matthew 6:14–15

As Christians we have no choice. We forfeit our fellowship with God and blessings here below when we don't forgive. If we have been forgiven of all our sins—and this includes even the sins we have forgotten about—how dare we withhold this from others?

Trying to Justify Our Sin

The mistake many of us make is this: we say openly and (seemingly) reasonably, "I know I am a sinner. I have done some pretty horrible things—but not as bad and horrible as that which they have done to me." This is a most common line, whether it is rape, child abuse, vicious lying, or infidelity. We say, "I would never rape, murder, or physically abuse anybody." Or we may say, "I may have stolen from that convenience store. I may have cheated on my income tax. I may even have gossiped a little. But I would never abuse a child." We may be among those who say, "I know what it is to lose my temper. I have been jealous at times. I have coveted someone else's success. But I've never done anything so wicked as to be unfaithful to my beloved spouse."

I understand this. Most of us have to forgive specific wrongs that we ourselves may well never do to another. But what we don't realize at first—and the truth may not be faced for a long time—is the meaning of Jesus's words that those of us who are unjust in that which is least will also be unjust in that which is much (Luke 16:10). Agree or disagree, that is Jesus's doctrine of sin. That is His view of people. The "little" sins we do that seem relatively harmless (taking a ballpoint pen from the office) only show what else we would do if we knew we would get away with it. The mild flirtation with the opposite sex is but the tip of the iceberg of what we would love to do—if we knew we wouldn't get caught.

The point is this: God knows not only the sins we have committed but also the sins of which we are capable. He knows our hearts. He sees what is deep down inside that we may not be willing to face. Our self-righteousness and personal sense of decency often camouflage the evil that is within our soul. When the Bible says in 1 John 1:7 that Jesus's blood purifies from *all sin*, it means we have been forgiven even for sins we weren't aware of. The truth is, given the right circumstances, pressure, temptation, and timing, *any* of us can match the evil (or its equivalent in God's sight) we ourselves have to forgive. If we deny this, it is because we don't agree with what the Bible says about men and women of any color, culture, education, or background.

And yet agreeing with the Bible doesn't make it easy. We are still indignant that this person—who knows the truth and should have known better—could carry out this deed or hurt us like that. But the Bible is saying that:

- ▹ We are guilty of a different sin that is just as heinous in God's eyes.
- ▹ We are capable of a sin just as bad in God's eyes.
- ▹ We may yet fall into such a sin as they did—or worse.

Not forgiving not only leads to deeper bitterness but also, as we have already seen, the capability of enacting a wrong that is worse than we ever dreamed of doing. God *could* judge us by allowing us eventually to fall into the exact same sin that we are required to forgive—should we dig our heels in and remain recalcitrant. I have certainly seen it happen. I know of people who were indignant over a particular conduct but who later did the very thing they criticized. This is why Jesus said, "Do not judge, or you too will be judged" (Matt. 7:1).

God nonetheless gives us motives for doing the right thing by appealing to our self-interest. He doesn't have to; He could say, "Just do it because I say so and because it is right." He could, but He doesn't. He could have said, "You have robbed

Me by withholding tithes. Start tithing now, because it is My law." He could have said that, but He didn't. He said, "'Bring the whole tithe into the storehouse, that there may be food in my house. Test me in this,' says the LORD Almighty, 'and see if I will not throw open the floodgates of heaven and pour out so much blessing that you will not have room enough for it'" (Mal. 3:10). In the same way, God appeals to us to do what is commanded and right—but in such a way as to encourage us to obey.

The Pragmatic Reasons for Forgiving

There are two pragmatic reasons to forgive:

1. Consider the consequences if you do forgive.

"Release them, and you will be released," Josif Tson said to me. I didn't think I could do it, but Josif was right. The bondage wasn't worth holding on to my unforgiveness. The absence of seeing Jesus's face wasn't worth it. The lack of peace wasn't worth it. But getting that old peace back (I had forgotten what it was like) was worth it all. God is a jealous God, and He won't let us enjoy this inner peace if we have an unforgiving spirit.

I remember when I first became aware that the old peace was gone. It was in August 1956. Less than a year before that I had what I like to call my own Damascus Road experience when driving in my car from Palmer to Nashville, Tennessee. The Lord Jesus Christ blessed me with such peace that I could not describe it were I Shakespeare, Wordsworth, and Shelley rolled into one. The peace was simply indescribable. But in August 1956 I lost my temper with my father. He accused me of recanting on what

I had been brought up to believe and said I was utterly out of God's will.

I completely "lost it," as they say. I shouldn't have, but I did. I felt so awful afterward. If only I could have asked him to forgive me for losing my temper (I didn't), and if only I had forgiven him for his well-meaning but untrue words (I didn't). Instead, I determined to spend the next few years vindicating myself. I might wish that Josif Tson had come alongside me at that time and warned me of the consequences of my bitterness. *If only*... All I know is, it was a long time before I found the key to the way back to peace.

> "Who knows how God will use you down the road if—once and for all—you set your enemies free and never look back?"

That's strange, isn't it? Here we have the plain words of Jesus in the Lord's Prayer, not to mention the rest of the New Testament. And I tried everything from tithing, double tithing, praying two hours a day, walking forward in a service any time I felt the urge, having some person lay hands on me, and so forth. But all I needed to do was to forgive my father—and an ever-increasing number of people who subsequently questioned me and the direction of my life.

If this book is tailor-made for you (because you are struggling to forgive and to overcome bitterness), consider the inner peace and the clear thinking that is closer than your fingertips, closer than the air you breathe. It is near you, even in your heart, but you are unable to experience it because of the resentment you are holding toward other people. Forgive them. Release them. Do it in your heart. Refuse those imaginary conversations that rob you of time and sleep. Think pleasant thoughts:

> Finally, brothers, whatever is true, whatever is noble, whatever is right, whatever is pure, whatever is lovely, whatever is admirable—if anything is excellent or praiseworthy—think about such things.
>
> —PHILIPPIANS 4:8

Stephen attained such a zenith of spirituality that his example played a part in the conversion of Saul of Tarsus (who was later renamed Paul). In immense pain from the stones that pummeled his body, Stephen managed to utter with his dying breath, "Lord, do not hold this sin against them" (Acts 7:60). Saul witnessed the whole incident and never forgot it. It can be so with us. "As it is written: 'No eye has seen, no ear has heard, no mind has conceived what God has prepared for those who love him'" (1 Cor. 2:9). Who knows how God will use you down the road if—once and for all—you set your enemies free and never look back?

2. Consider the consequences if you don't forgive.

Jesus put this very strongly indeed: "But if you do not forgive men their sins, your Father will not forgive your sins" (Matt. 6:15). That doesn't mean you won't be guided or looked after. God still guided and looked after me. But now I realize why I lost so much that I had once had. Great though God's plans for me may have been, He didn't bend the rules for me. He allowed me to get deep into debt and suffer the humiliation of having to be out of the full-time preaching ministry; I peddled vacuum cleaners as a door-to-door salesman for years, living under a cloud whereby nobody believed in me and having a godly father believe all he feared most concerning me.

Whether I hurt my health in all this, I can't say. But in some cases the refusal to forgive leads to countless physical ailments. Lack of forgiveness is aging; it puts lines on faces before they should come. In some cases it means sleeplessness.

Having to forgive my father is not what was at hand when I had my aforementioned encounter with Josif Tson, for my friendship with Josif came many years later. But what is true is this: not forgiving my father made it easy and natural to be bitter later. The person who became like a substitute father (I turned to someone else for approval) hurt me even more than my father had—and the bitterness toward him was a thousand times worse. But I felt no conviction that this was wrong. Neither did God manifest Himself in any great power. I forfeited anointing that could have been mine, though.

The consequences of an unforgiving spirit add up to one thing: the bitterness isn't worth it. The devil does not want you to forgive others; he loves it when you are bitter. This way he has access to you. He therefore will put up what appear to be good reasons for wanting your adversary to be punished—and by you if at all possible. Those imaginary conversations are inspired by him, by the way. He wants to rob you of time, energy, and joy. You can expect obstacles to be put in your way if you try to forgive. They will seem "providential"—excuses why you are the exception to the rule. Never forget that when Jonah decided to run from God and head for Tarshish, he found (providentially!) a ship that was going there (Jon. 1:3). It seemed at the time that God was behind his decisions. So you too will find ways and reasons why you need not forgive, but the consequences of this are disastrous.

Steps in Totally Forgiving Others

Since forgiveness is a choice, what is the next step? If we are persuaded that it is right and have decided to do it (and not look back), what next? The answer has already been given in chapter two, but I restate the reasons here.

1. Make the deliberate and irrevocable choice not to tell anyone what they did.

(As I said earlier, you may need to do this for therapeutic reasons, but only to one person who in turn will never reveal your heart.) Jesus also said that the one who is faithful in the least thing is faithful also in much, and this is the first thing. Do not mention it; refuse to tell anybody.

This isn't necessarily easy sometimes, but when our motive is to hurt another person by telling on them, there is sin on our part. So do not tell it at all or in part; keep it quiet.

2. Be pleasant to them should you be around them.

Do not say or do anything that would make them anxious. Put them at their ease.

This can be hard to do, certainly harder than the first step. It is we who are afraid when we can't forgive. When we pass our fear to them, it is utterly the opposite of what Jesus would do. He would say, "Fear not." Josif Tson says that there are 366 statements of "Do not fear" (or the equivalent) in the Bible—"One for every day of the year and one for leap year!" he says. God does not want us to fear; we must not do or say anything to cause others to fear. Be nice. Put them at ease. This is what Jesus did when He turned up after His resurrection to ten disciples behind closed doors. (See John 20:19.)

3. If conversation ensues, say that which would set them free from guilt.

Guilt is most painful, and we can easily punish people by sending them on a "guilt trip." Never do that. Remember that Jesus doesn't want us to feel guilty. When we are going to be Jesus to another, then we will not want them to be angry with themselves.

This is a hard one. We get some satisfaction when we think they feel really, really bad. That defuses us and eases our anger somewhat. But if we want to be valiant and utterly magnanimous—thus showing true godliness—we will say whatever is the equivalent of Joseph's words: "Do not be angry with yourselves" (Gen. 45:5). Joseph would not allow his brothers to feel guilty, and this is a choice we too must make. It's hard, but it is what we would want if things were reversed and we needed forgiveness. "Do to others as you would have them do to you" (Luke 6:31).

4. Let them feel good about themselves.

Not only does this mean *never* reminding them of their wrong and your hurt, but it also means helping them through any guilt they may have. This can be done without any reference to what they did. If it is not in the open, as with Joseph's situation, that is of course different; he let his brothers save face by showing God's sovereign strategy in their sin. But in many cases you will not be able to talk about anything specifically. You can still let them save face, because you know that they know what they did.

You therefore must behave as though you don't even think they did anything wrong! That is hard for all of us, but it must be done. Say whatever you can (as long as it is true) that will give that person a sense of dignity. That is the point of Galatians 6:1: "Brothers, if someone is caught in a sin, you who are spiritual should restore him gently. But watch yourself, or you also may be tempted." As long as there is a trace of self-righteousness and pointing the finger, your attempt at total forgiveness will backfire.

5. Protect them from their greatest fear.

If you are aware of some deep, dark secret and fear they have, they will probably know that you know. If they can tell by your graciousness that their secret will never be revealed—ever—to anyone, they will be relieved. You only tell them when you know they know what you know, and you are convinced this would make them feel better. If by reminding them it would obviously not make them feel better, don't even come close!

Remember that Joseph knew his brothers' greatest fear was that their father, Jacob, would learn the truth of their evil deed. Joseph never mentioned this directly but suggested they speak to Jacob in such a way that they wouldn't have to tell him after all. (See Genesis 45:9–13.) It must have given the brothers incalculable relief to know that they were not obliged to tell Jacob. But that is what total forgiveness is all about: setting people free.

6. Keep it up today, tomorrow, this year, and next.

As we have said, total forgiveness is a lifelong commitment. Some days will be easier than others. There will come a time when you think you are completely over it and have won a total victory—only to find the very next day Satan reminds you of what they did and the utter injustice that they will be unpunished and never exposed. The temptation to bitterness will emerge. After all, we're not perfect! If we say we have no sin—that we are incapable of the same old bitterness—we are deceived (1 John 1:8).

This is exactly why I read Luke 6:37 every day: "Do not judge, and you will not be judged. Do not condemn, and you will not be condemned. Forgive, and you will be forgiven." All commitments to forgive need renewal. In my case, daily. I am not telling you that this is what *you* must do, but be warned: the devil is cunning. He will come through the back door unexpectedly and try to upset you for forgiving. When you forgave your enemy, you then and there removed that open invitation to the devil to get inside. Satan's favorite rationale is bitterness—he therefore will keep trying to get back into your thought life.

Whether it be Luke 6:37 or another way forward in your case—even if you aren't required to keep it up each day—I can tell you right now that it is only a matter of time before your commitment to forgive will need to be renewed.

7. Pray for them.

"But I tell you: Love your enemies and pray for those who persecute you" (Matt. 5:44). When you do this from the heart—praying for their being blessed and off the hook—you're there. It is not a perfunctory prayer, not a "We commit them to You" prayer, and certainly not an "Oh God, please deal with them" prayer. It is praying that God will forgive them—that is, *overlook* what they have done and bless and prosper them as though they'd never sinned at all.

But as John Calvin said, doing this is "exceedingly difficult." As Chrysostom said, it is the very highest summit of self-control. "Better a patient man than a warrior, a man who controls his temper than one who takes a city" (Prov. 16:32).

Praying for the one who has hurt you or let you down is the greatest challenge of all, for three reasons:

- ▹ You take a route utterly against the flesh.
- ▹ Nobody will ever know you are doing it.
- ▹ Your heart could break when God answers that prayer and truly blesses them as if they'd never sinned.

And yet Jesus's word to pray for such people is not a polite suggestion; it is a command—and one that may seem so outrageous that you want to dismiss it out of hand. Some see it as a lofty but unrealistic goal.

I remember a church leader turning to me to pray about his son-in-law who had been unfaithful to the leader's daughter. He said to me that his own prayer was only this: that God would "deal" with this man. "This is where I have come to," he said to me, "that God will deal with him."

I understood what he meant, and I felt for him. I find what people do to our own offspring the hardest things to forgive. I therefore understood what he was feeling. A few days later it was reported that this leader's son-in-law had been in a serious accident. This same church leader was on the phone, glad that the accident had happened. Now in this particular case there was nothing sinister in this euphoria. He simply hoped that the accident would wake up his son-in-law to put his marriage back together. It was so understandable.

But this is not what Jesus means. He is commanding us to pray that our enemy will be *blessed*. If, however, you should pray that they will be cursed or punished instead of being blessed, just remember that is how your enemy possibly feels about you. After all, have *you* ever been someone's enemy? Have *you* ever done something that brought a fellow Christian to tears and brokenness? If so, how would you like that person to pray for *you*? That God will deal with *you*? That God will cause *you* to have an accident? Yet how would it make you feel if they prayed that you would be blessed and let off the hook? That you would prosper as if you'd never sinned? Would you not like that? "Do to others as you would have them do to you" (Luke 6:31).

Jesus wants a sincere prayer from us. It is like signing your name to a document, having it witnessed, and never looking back. You are not allowed to tell the world, "Guess what I did? I have actually prayed for my unfaithful spouse to be blessed." No. It is quiet. Only the angels witness it, but it makes God very happy.

After all, every parent wants their children to get along with one another. No parent likes it when one child comes and squeals on the other and demands that they be punished. The poor parent is put on the spot. What gladdens the heart of every parent is when there is love and forgiveness, and the parent is not put on the spot to have to take sides and punish anyone. That is what we do for God when we ask that He bless and not curse. He told us to pray for our enemies, "that you may be sons of your Father in heaven. He causes his sun to rise on the evil and the good, and sends rain on the righteous and the unrighteousness" (Matt. 5:45).

The Five Stages in Praying for Our Enemies

There are five stages, or levels, of praying for one's enemy:

- ▷ **Duty**. The first level is strictly based on obedience; you are doing it because you feel you have to.
- ▷ **Debt**. You have reached the second level when you are so conscious of what you have been forgiven of that you cannot help but pray for your enemy. You do not want God to "spill the beans" on you, so you pray that your enemy too will be spared.
- ▷ **Desire**. You begin to pray for your enemy, because it is what you really want.
- ▷ **Delight**. This takes desire a step further. It is when you love doing it! You get joy from praying for and blessing your enemies.
- ▷ **Durability**. This means that what you took on as a lifelong commitment becomes a lifestyle. The thought of turning back or praying in a different way is out of the question. It has become a habit, and it no longer

seems like something extraordinary. Jackie Pullinger said, "To the spiritual person the supernatural seems natural." What began as a duty and once seemed insurmountable is now almost second nature.

> "Another surprising consequence of your prayer is that—just maybe—your enemy may become your friend."

All this is done in secret, behind the scenes. Only the angels know. It is quiet intercession. You aren't allowed to get your reward or applause from people who may think, "Oh, isn't that lovely you would pray for your enemy like that!" No. It is a secret that must never be told. Enter into your place of prayer and shut the door behind you. "Then your Father, who sees what is done in secret, will reward you" (Matt. 6:4).

There are several consequences of praying for your enemies or persons who have disappointed you. The most obvious consequence is your reward in heaven. But another consequence is that—be warned—God may answer your prayer! "Oh, no!" you may say, "I only prayed for them because I was being obedient. Surely God would not actually bless and prosper that wicked person?" Well, He may indeed! The question is: Will you still pray the prayer?

Let's turn the tables around and assume you have hurt somebody. If they prayed for your prosperity, you wouldn't object, would you? How do you know this hasn't already happened? How do you know that the blessing and fulfillment you are experiencing are not the answer to prayer on your behalf by someone who has been hurt by you? You may say, "They would never pray for me like that." Perhaps. But the very fact that you are blessed and yet have caused hurt in someone else's life is proof that God hasn't chosen to throw the book at you yet. Be thankful for that, and pray for your enemies in return.

Another surprising consequence of your prayer is that—just maybe—your enemy may become your friend. That is what God did to us:

> God was reconciling the world to himself in Christ, not counting men's sins against them. And he has committed to us the message of reconciliation.
>
> —2 CORINTHIANS 5:19

You too may well win your enemy over by loving them and praying for them. "I don't want this person as a friend," you may say now. That's OK. We saw earlier that total forgiveness does not always mean reconciliation. Do not feel guilty if you don't want to become close friends. But in some cases this has happened. And if there is a reconciliation or a friendship that eventually results, that person may say to you, "You were brilliant the whole time. You were loving and caring, never vindictive." One rule of thumb to follow: treat your enemy now the way you will be glad you did should you become good friends.

The greatest positive consequence is the knowledge that you have pleased God. I want to be like Enoch, who was "commended as one who pleased God" (Heb. 11:5). Nothing pleases God more than our loving and praying for our enemies. It is significant that Job's troubles stopped when he prayed for his friends who were persecutors and tormentors during his suffering. "After Job had prayed for his friends, the LORD made him prosperous again and gave him twice as much as he had before" (Job 42:10).

Doing this is, of course, our duty—but it eventually becomes a delight. If you hate, you will give your enemy your heart and mind. As Nelson Mandela said, don't give those two things away.

CONCLUSION

Margaret Moss, whose husband, Norman, was the minister of the Queen's Road Baptist Church in Wimbledon, has given me permission to share the following two stories. I learned of them when I asked her if she had seen any healings take place lately. She gave two recent examples, and both, as it happens, pertained to the theme of this book.

The first concerned a woman who had been in a car accident twenty-two years before. Her neck had been in constant pain for all these years, and because she could not turn her head to be able to look into the rearview mirror of her car, she had been forced to forfeit her driver's license. Margaret asked her if she had ever prayed for the driver of the car who had caused the accident.

"No," was her reply.

Margaret suggested that the woman pray for him.

"I forgive him," the lady began to pray.

"Now bless him," Margaret continued.

The woman began to bless this man, and the pain left. The next morning she could move her neck for the first time in twenty-two years. That was more than a year ago, and the healing has continued.

The second account involved a lady in her forties whose father had terribly abused her. This lady claimed that she had said to the Lord, "I forgive him," again and again. But despite her prayer, she had continued in "heaviness of spirit," said Margaret. "I then suggested that she begin blessing her father as well as speaking the words that she had forgiven him. The moment she said, 'I bless my father,' she went ballistic!"

"Forgiveness is not total forgiveness until we bless our enemies—and pray for them to be blessed."

The heaviness completely left! The last time Margaret saw this lady, she said that the spirit of heaviness was still gone. The lady added, "Now my life has completely changed."

Forgiveness is not *total* forgiveness until we bless our enemies—and pray for them to be blessed. Forgiving them is a major step; *totally* forgiving them has fully been achieved when we set God free to bless them. But in this, we are the first to be blessed, and those who totally forgive are blessed the most.

In the introduction to this book we noted that the teaching and carrying out of forgiveness has been recognized as valid and therapeutic even outside the realm of the Christian faith. You will recall the *Daily Express* article about the course in Leeds.[1] The reason for this course, which was paid for by a grant from the John Templeton Foundation, was apparently the belief that forgiveness can be good for your health. Holding a grudge, it is said, leads to illnesses ranging from common colds to heart disease because of all the stored-up anger and stress. Dr. Sandi Mann, a psychologist at the University of Central Lancashire, believes that there is a strong link between our emotions and our immune system. All of this goes to show the benefits of forgiving people—even if we were not motivated by Jesus and the New Testament!

Here are ten steps to freedom, as found in the *Daily Express* article:

1. Stop excusing, pardoning, or rationalizing.

2. Pinpoint the actions that have hurt you.

3. Spend time thinking of ways in which your life would be more satisfying if you could let go of your grievances.

4. Try replacing angry thoughts about the "badness" of the perpetrator with thoughts about how the offender is also a human being who is vulnerable to harm.

5. Identify with the offender's probable state of mind. Understand the perpetrator's history while not condoning their actions.

6. Spend some time developing greater compassion toward the perpetrator.

7. Become more aware that you have needed other people's forgiveness in the past.

8. Make a heartfelt resolution not to pass on your own pain.

9. Spend time appreciating the sense of purpose and direction that comes after steps 1–8.

10. Enjoy the sense of emotional relief that comes when the burden of a grudge has melted away. Enjoy also the feeling of goodwill and mercy you have shown.

“If certain things were true under the Mosaic Law, how much more is promised now that Christ has come and fulfilled it?”

There is a wonderful phrase in the Book of Hebrews, “How much more…” (Heb. 9:14; 10:29). The point the writer is making is that if certain things were true under the Mosaic Law, how much more is promised now that Christ has come and fulfilled it?

It seems to me that if the secular world is catching on to the teachings of Jesus—even if they are not acknowledging Him or the Holy Spirit—and deriving benefits from that teaching, *how much more* should Christians experience this? If non-Christians can find peace because it is better for their health, *how much more* should you and I—who want to please God and honor the Holy Spirit—embrace this teaching with all our hearts? It surely leaves us all without excuse.

The most profound thing I ever heard Joni Eareckson Tada say is this: “I am a Christian not because of what it does for me but because it is true.” We should believe Christ’s teaching because it is true.

But it also works. Let the past be past—at last.

NOTES

Introduction

1. Susan Pape, "Can You Learn to Forgive?" *Daily Express*, June 5, 2000.

2. John Wesley, "I Felt My Heart Strangely Warmed," as viewed at St. Michael's College, Vermont, http://academics.smcvt.edu/relstudies_courses/RS130/John%20Wesley.htm (accessed April 16, 2007).

3. Gary Thomas, "The Forgiveness Factor," *Christianity Today*, vol. 44, no. 1 (10 January 2000): 38.

4. Ibid.

5. Ibid.

Chapter 1
What Is Total Forgiveness?

1. Corrie ten Boom, *The Hiding Place* (Boston: G. K. Hall, 1973).

2. William Shakespeare, *Othello*, 3.3.183–187. Reference is to act, scene, and lines.

Chapter 2
How to Know We Have Totally Forgiven

1. Dale Carnegie, *How to Win Friends and Influence People* (New York: Simon and Schuster, 1937).

Chapter 3
The Lord's Prayer and Forgiveness

1. "In Evil Long I Took Delight" by John Newton. Public domain.

Chapter 6
The Art of Forgiving and Forgetting

1. "Jim and Tammy Faye Return to TV," *Larry King Live*, episode aired May 29, 2000. Transcript obtained from Internet: www.cnn.com/TRANSCRIPTS/0005/29/lkl.00.html.

Chapter 7
How to Forgive—Totally

1. "Jim and Tammy Faye Return to TV," *Larry King Live*.
2. "How Firm a Foundation," from John Rippon's Selection of Hymns, 1787. Public domain.

Conclusion

1. Pape, "Can You Learn to Forgive?"

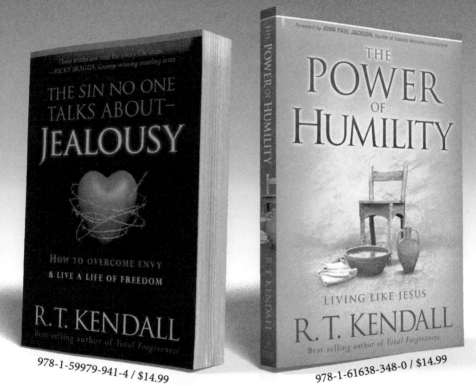